P9-DXO-296

America's Greatest
New Cooks

FOOD&WINE

FOOD & WINE
AMERICA'S GREATEST NEW COOKS VOL. 1
EDITOR IN CHIEF **Dana Cowin**
EXECUTIVE EDITOR **Kate Heddings**
DESIGNER **Michelle Leong**
EDITOR **Susan Choung**
FEATURES EDITOR **Michael Endelman**
ASSOCIATE FOOD EDITOR **Justin Chapple**
ASSOCIATE WINE EDITOR **Megan Krigbaum**
COPY EDITOR **Lisa Leventer**
RESEARCHER **Michelle Loayza**
PRODUCTION MANAGER **Matt Carson**
DIRECTOR OF PHOTOGRAPHY **Fredrika Stjärne**
DEPUTY PHOTO EDITOR **Anthony LaSala**
ASSOCIATE PHOTO EDITOR **Sara Parks**
CONTRIBUTING WRITERS **M. Elizabeth Sheldon, Jane Sigal**

FOOD PHOTOGRAPHER **Christina Holmes**
FOOD STYLIST **Vivian Lui**
PROP STYLIST **Pamela Duncan Silver**
PORTRAIT & INTERIOR PHOTOGRAPHERS **See page 255.**

FOOD & WINE MAGAZINE

SVP / EDITOR IN CHIEF **Dana Cowin**
CREATIVE DIRECTOR **Stephen Scoble**
MANAGING EDITOR **Mary Ellen Ward**
EXECUTIVE EDITOR **Pamela Kaufman**
EXECUTIVE FOOD EDITOR **Tina Ujlaki**
ART DIRECTOR **Courtney Waddell Eckersley**

ISBN: 978-1-932624-56-4

Published by American Express Publishing Corporation
1120 Avenue of the Americas, New York, New York 10036

Manufactured in the United States of America

AMERICAN EXPRESS PUBLISHING CORPORATION
PRESIDENT / CHIEF EXECUTIVE OFFICER **Ed Kelly**
CHIEF MARKETING OFFICER / PRESIDENT,
   DIGITAL MEDIA **Mark V. Stanich**
SVP / CHIEF FINANCIAL OFFICER **Paul B. Francis**
VPs / GENERAL MANAGERS **Frank Bland, Keith Strohmeier**

VP, BOOKS & PRODUCTS / PUBLISHER **Marshall Corey**
DIRECTOR, BOOK PROGRAMS **Bruce Spanier**
SENIOR MARKETING MANAGER, BRANDED BOOKS **Eric Lucie**
ASSISTANT MARKETING MANAGER **Stacy Mallis**
DIRECTOR OF FULFILLMENT & PREMIUM VALUE **Philip Black**
MANAGER OF CUSTOMER EXPERIENCE
   & PRODUCT DEVELOPMENT **Betsy Wilson**
DIRECTOR OF FINANCE **Thomas Noonan**
ASSOCIATE BUSINESS MANAGER **Uma Mahabir**
OPERATIONS DIRECTOR (PREPRESS) **Rosalie Abatemarco Samat**
OPERATIONS DIRECTOR (MANUFACTURING) **Anthony White**
SENIOR MANAGER, CONTRACTS & RIGHTS **Jeniqua Moore**

FRONT COVER

PHOTOGRAPHER (ASPARAGUS, MEATBALLS, PASTA, CHEESECAKE)
   Christina Holmes
PHOTOGRAPHER (WHISK) **Peden + Munk**
PHOTOGRAPHER (BREAD) **Michael Turek**
PHOTOGRAPHER (JARS) **Eric Wolfinger**
PHOTOGRAPHER (PIGS) **Daniel Shea**

BACK COVER

PHOTOGRAPHER (FOOD) **Christina Holmes**
PHOTOGRAPHER (PIZZA PEEL) **Corey Hendrickson**
PHOTOGRAPHER (CHISELS) **Eric Wolfinger**

INSIDE FLAP

PHOTOGRAPHER **Huge Galdones**

America's Greatest New Cooks

SPECTACULAR RECIPES WITH FRESH IDEAS FROM TOMORROW'S STARS

FOOD&**WINE**
BOOKS

American Express Publishing Corporation, New York

CONTENTS

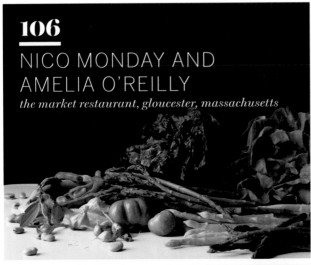

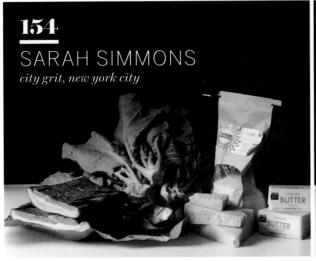

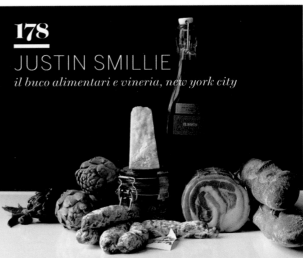

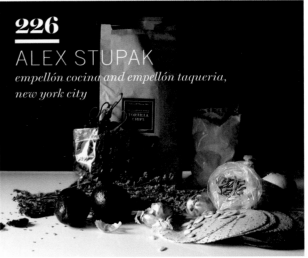

THE RECIPES

starters

pasta & grains

fish & shellfish

FOREWORD

as editors at food & wine, we search the world for great eating experiences. But once in a while we have a meal that's more than great: It's game-changing. Recently, for instance, a few of us made our way to the Purple Pig in Chicago, curious about a renegade young chef named Jimmy Bannos, Jr. The menu was so sprawling that even deciding what to get was a challenge. We did what we always do, which is order too much of everything. Soon Bannos's signature salad arrived: crispy pig's ears with kale, pickled cherry peppers and a fried egg, all served in a little ceramic piggy. Bannos isn't the only nose-to-tail, pork-obsessed chef in America, but those pig's ears were unforgettable. And dish after dish (including, surprisingly, all the vegetable sides) confirmed that Bannos is a superstar in the making.

This book is all about these superstars of tomorrow. They are an incredibly diverse group, ranging from brilliant chefs cooking Mexican, Italian, Middle Eastern and Asian cuisine to bakers crafting Parisian-style pastries in rural Vermont. There's even an ambitious home cook turned pop-up restaurateur. We captured their intensity and vision in pictures from some of the most acclaimed photographers in America. And we collected their simplest, most delicious recipes, from pasta in a luscious tomato-almond pesto (page 192) to fudgy chocolate cookies (page 98) that are the best you will ever taste.

We hope the talented people and the fabulous recipes in this book inspire you to make your own discoveries, both out in the world and inside your kitchen.

Dana Cowin
Editor in Chief
FOOD & WINE Magazine

Pete Heddings
Executive Editor
FOOD & WINE Cookbooks

NICOLAUS BALLA

CHEF • BAR TARTINE • SAN FRANCISCO

it's become commonplace for chefs to make their own charcuterie, pickles and condiments, but Bar Tartine's chef Nicolaus Balla takes the artisanal, DIY ethos to another level: In the course of a year he dries thousands of pounds of local peppers to make paprika and ferments 400-pound batches of sauerkraut. At his restaurant in San Francisco's Mission District, there is salami curing in the basement and tubs of homemade yogurt and sour cream in the reach-in refrigerator. It's all part of Balla's commitment to preserving authentic cooking techniques while updating centuries-old recipes—a style he calls "new Old World."

At Bar Tartine—the restaurant owned by Chad Robertson and Elisabeth Prueitt of the cult favorite Tartine Bakery in San Francisco—Balla reinterprets the humble, hearty food of eastern and northern Europe, incorporating Californian and Japanese influences. For instance, he prepares a Czech-inspired steak tartare with supertender wagyu beef, house-made apricot ketchup and pickles to serve with caraway bread from Tartine Bakery. "Nick concentrates ancient flavors—for example, pickling and smoking food—then lightens them with local produce," says Robertson. "He innovates while never losing sight of the foundations of cooking and flavor."

Though he was born in rural Michigan, Balla spent his high school years living with his father outside Budapest. They shared a house with a Hungarian family that slaughtered pigs in their backyard. "I got a real taste for Hungarian food: the bread, sausage and cheese," Balla says. He returned to the United States and attended the Culinary Institute of America in Hyde Park, New York, in 2000, eventually cooking Cal-Japanese food at Ozumo and O Izakaya in San Francisco. These experiences opened his eyes to the way that fermented, aged and preserved ingredients like *kombu* (dried kelp) and *katsuobushi* (smoked, fermented and dried bonito flakes) can add intense, supercharged flavor to food.

In 2009, Balla opened his own Cal-Japanese spot, Nombe. But when Robertson, a regular customer at Nombe, found out about Balla's Hungarian background, he convinced him to move over to Bar Tartine. "Even though he was doing something totally different, we were coming from the same place," says Robertson. "Nick is authentic and progressive at the same time."

Balla and Robertson traveled to Scandinavia to explore ancient-grain breads for Tartine Bakery, then to Budapest to research Hungarian cuisine for Balla's new Bar Tartine menu, which launched in early 2011. "It was a risk transforming Bar Tartine, which had been a beloved California bistro, into this weird eastern European whatever-it-is," Balla says. Inspired by the trip, Balla finesses Hungarian classics like sour cherry soup, adding fennel to make it more savory (page 22); for chicken *paprikás*, he thickens the sauce with chicken skin and potato instead of flour to create a silkier gravy rich with chicken flavor (page 28). His sausage and sauerkraut soup, based on the Slovak Christmas soup called *kapustnica*, includes untraditional ingredients like serrano chiles and shiitake mushrooms (page 30). He dresses roasted brussels sprouts with cilantro, lime and caraway seeds (page 18)—one foot in Asia, the other in eastern Europe.

Even in an era when it seems like chefs have explored every possible cross-cultural combination, Balla's food feels original. Says Robertson, "I could pick his dishes out of a lineup."

11

"**Nick concentrates ancient flavors, then lightens them with local produce. He innovates and continues to evolve while never losing sight of the foundations of cooking and flavor.**

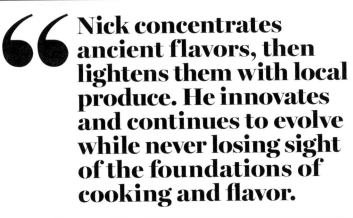

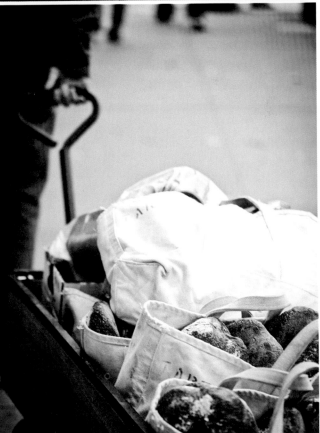

This simple eastern European–style salad has been one of Balla's favorites ever since he lived in Hungary as a teenager. He marinates sweet roasted beets in a red wine vinaigrette to make them more flavorful before tossing them with scallions, herbs and crumbled blue cheese.

BEET & BLUE CHEESE SALAD

ACTIVE *30 min*   **TOTAL** *2 hr 30 min*   **MAKES** *8 servings*

3   pounds medium beets
¼   cup grapeseed oil, plus more
    for brushing
Kosher salt and freshly ground
    black pepper
2   tablespoons fresh lemon juice
2   tablespoons red wine vinegar
1   teaspoon light brown sugar
1   garlic clove, minced
3   scallions, white and light green
    parts only, thinly sliced
1   tablespoon finely chopped dill
1   tablespoon finely chopped parsley
4   ounces firm cow-milk blue
    cheese, such as Point Reyes
    Original Blue, crumbled

1 Preheat the oven to 350°. In a small baking dish, brush the beets with oil and season with salt and pepper. Cover the baking dish tightly with foil and roast the beets for about 1 hour and 15 minutes, until tender when pierced with a knife. Let cool, then peel the beets and cut them into 1-inch wedges.

2 In a large bowl, whisk the ¼ cup of grapeseed oil with the lemon juice, vinegar, sugar and garlic; season with salt and pepper. Add the beets, toss to coat and let them stand at room temperature for 30 minutes.

3 Add the scallions, dill and parsley to the beets and toss well. Transfer the beets to plates, top with the crumbled blue cheese and serve.

SERVE WITH *Good-quality brown or black bread.*

MAKE AHEAD *The marinated beets can be refrigerated for up to 2 days. Top with the cheese just before serving.*

For this spicy, hummus-inspired vegan spread, Balla uses the sunflower, an abundant crop in Hungary, in three forms: the seeds, the oil and the sweet, crunchy tuber of the sunchoke (a variety of sunflower). The result is an unusual, nutty and luscious spread that's fantastic with fresh vegetables.

TRIPLE SUNFLOWER SPREAD WITH CRUDITÉS VINAIGRETTE

ACTIVE *40 min*　**TOTAL** *1 hr*　**MAKES** *6 servings*

SPREAD

　6　ounces sunchokes
　　　(Jerusalem artichokes), scrubbed
　¼　cup plus 2 tablespoons
　　　sunflower oil
Kosher salt and freshly ground black
　　　pepper
　½　cup finely chopped onion
　2　garlic cloves, minced
　1　cup roasted unsalted shelled
　　　sunflower seeds (6 ounces)
　2　tablespoons fresh lemon juice
　2　teaspoons hot Hungarian paprika
　1　serrano chile, seeded and chopped
　1　teaspoon onion powder
　1　teaspoon honey

VEGETABLES

　3　tablespoons sunflower oil
　1　tablespoon fresh lemon juice
　1　tablespoon red wine vinegar
　1　teaspoon light brown sugar
　½　teaspoon finely chopped oregano
Kosher salt and freshly ground
　　　black pepper
Sliced tomatoes, grape tomatoes,
　　　Hungarian wax peppers,
　　　bell peppers, cucumbers and
　　　scallions, for serving

1 MAKE THE SPREAD Preheat the oven to 375°. On a rimmed baking sheet, toss the sunchokes with 1 tablespoon of the oil and season with salt and pepper. Roast for about 30 minutes, until tender; let cool completely.

2 Meanwhile, in a small skillet, heat 1 tablespoon of the oil. Add the onion and garlic and cook over moderate heat until softened and just starting to brown, about 7 minutes. Scrape the onion and garlic into a food processor and let cool.

3 Add the sunflower seeds and the cooled sunchokes to the food processor and puree. Add the lemon juice, paprika, serrano, onion powder, honey and the remaining ¼ cup of oil and puree until nearly smooth; season with salt and pepper. Scrape the spread into a bowl.

4 PREPARE THE VEGETABLES In a small bowl, whisk the oil with the lemon juice, vinegar, sugar and oregano; season with salt and pepper. Arrange the vegetables on plates or a platter, drizzle the vinaigrette on top and serve with the sunflower spread.

MAKE AHEAD *The sunflower spread can be refrigerated for up to 2 days. Bring to room temperature before serving.*

These roasted, caramelized brussels sprouts are a popular fall and winter dish at Bar Tartine. Balla tosses them in a sweet-tart dressing with cilantro, mint and chiles—flavors that evoke Southeast Asia. The caraway seeds connect the dish to eastern Europe.

WARM BRUSSELS SPROUTS WITH HONEY, CARAWAY & LIME

ACTIVE *20 min*   **TOTAL** *1 hr*   **MAKES** *4 to 6 servings*

2 pounds brussels sprouts, halved lengthwise
3 tablespoons extra-virgin olive oil
Kosher salt
¼ teaspoon caraway seeds
One ¼-inch piece of star anise
¼ cup shredded carrot
2 tablespoons fresh lime juice
2 tablespoons honey
1 small garlic clove, minced
¼ cup thinly sliced scallions
¼ cup chopped mint
¼ cup chopped cilantro
2 serrano chiles, seeded and thinly sliced

1 Preheat the oven to 425°. In a large bowl, toss the brussels sprouts with the olive oil and season with salt. Spread on a large rimmed baking sheet and roast for about 40 minutes, stirring once or twice, until the brussels sprouts are tender and crisp on the edges.

2 Meanwhile, in a small skillet, toast the caraway seeds and star anise until fragrant, about 1 minute. Transfer to a spice grinder and let cool completely, then grind to a fine powder.

3 In a small bowl, whisk the carrot with the lime juice, honey, garlic and the spice powder. In the large bowl, toss the hot brussels sprouts with the dressing, scallions, mint, cilantro and chiles and season with salt. Serve right away.

"I like to call this a spoon salad," Balla says, "because it's like a soup and a salad in one dish. You want to eat it with a spoon and a huge loaf of bread next to you." He lets the salami and cheese sit with the vegetables for at least an hour. This creates juices at the bottom of the bowl—perfect for dipping bread.

HUNGARIAN CHOPPED SALAD

ACTIVE *20 min*   **TOTAL** *1 hr 20 min*   **MAKES** *6 to 8 servings*

- ½ pound paprika salami (see Note), dry chorizo or Calabrese salami, halved lengthwise and thinly sliced crosswise
- ½ pound Havarti cheese, cut into ½-inch dice
- 2 cups white mushrooms, sliced ¼ inch thick
- 2 Persian cucumbers, sliced ¼ inch thick
- 2 medium tomatoes, cut into ½-inch dice, or 1½ cups halved cherry tomatoes
- 2 Hungarian wax peppers, thinly sliced
- 4 scallions, white and light green parts only, chopped
- ½ small red onion, finely diced
- 2 tablespoons red wine vinegar
- 2 tablespoons finely chopped cilantro
- 1 tablespoon sweet Hungarian paprika
- 1 teaspoon brown sugar
- 1 garlic clove, minced
- 1 teaspoon kosher salt
- ½ teaspoon freshly ground black pepper

In a large bowl, combine all of the salad ingredients and toss well. Cover the salad and refrigerate for at least 1 hour, tossing every 15 minutes. Season the salad with additional salt and black pepper and serve at room temperature.

NOTE *Paprika salami is a traditional Hungarian dry salami flavored with paprika and garlic. It can be found at specialty food shops and hungariandeli.com.*

MAKE AHEAD *The salad can be refrigerated overnight.*

Traditional Hungarian chilled sour cherry soup is sweet enough to be a dessert. Balla blends fennel into his more savory version and serves the beautiful pink soup as a first course at Bar Tartine. "Fennel might be my favorite vegetable," he says.

CHILLED SOUR CHERRY SOUP WITH FENNEL & SOUR CREAM

ACTIVE *30 min*   **TOTAL** *1 hr 30 min*   **MAKES** *6 to 8 servings*

2 tablespoons sunflower or grapeseed oil, plus more for drizzling
1 cup finely chopped onion
1 cup finely chopped fennel bulb (½ pound)
1 garlic clove, minced
Kosher salt and freshly ground black pepper
1 pound fresh or frozen sour cherries, pitted, plus more for garnish
¾ cup buttermilk
½ cup sour cream
1 tablespoon sugar
Chopped dill and parsley, for garnish

1 In a medium saucepan, heat the 2 tablespoons of oil. Add the onion, fennel, garlic and a generous pinch each of salt and pepper and cook over moderately low heat until the vegetables are softened, 8 to 10 minutes. Transfer the vegetables to a blender and let cool.

2 Add the 1 pound of sour cherries, the buttermilk, sour cream, sugar and ½ cup of water to the blender and puree until smooth; season with salt and pepper. Transfer to a large bowl, cover and refrigerate until well chilled, at least 1 hour.

3 Ladle the soup into bowls and drizzle lightly with oil. Garnish with dill, parsley and a few cherries and serve.

MAKE AHEAD *The soup can be refrigerated overnight.*

These tartines *(open-face sandwiches) are Balla's take on Danish* smørrebrød. *He gives them an upgrade with a lush potato–sour cream sauce flavored with dill, parsley and horseradish.*

SMOKED TROUT TARTINES WITH POTATO-DILL SAUCE

TOTAL *45 min*   **MAKES** *8 servings*

1 large baking potato, peeled
   and cut into 1-inch pieces
1 cup sour cream
2 tablespoons mayonnaise
1 tablespoon fresh lemon juice
1 garlic clove, minced
2 tablespoons finely chopped dill,
   plus more for garnish
2 tablespoons finely chopped
   parsley, plus more for garnish
1 teaspoon finely grated fresh
   horseradish, plus more for serving
Kosher salt and freshly ground
   black pepper
Extra-virgin olive oil, for frying
   and drizzling
1 large shallot, halved lengthwise
   and thinly sliced crosswise
8 slices of dark rye bread
6 ounces skinless smoked trout
   fillet, flaked (or smoked salmon,
   cut into 2-inch strips)

PAIR WITH *Crisp, dry lager:*
Lagunitas Pils

1 In a small saucepan, cover the potato with water and bring to a boil. Simmer over moderate heat until tender, about 10 minutes. Drain and pass the potato through a ricer into a bowl; let cool completely. Measure out 1 cup of the mashed potato; reserve the rest for another use.

2 In a medium bowl, whisk the sour cream with the mayonnaise, lemon juice, garlic and the 1 cup of mashed potato. Whisk in the 2 tablespoons each of dill and parsley and the 1 teaspoon of horseradish; season the potato-dill sauce with salt and pepper.

3 In a small skillet, heat ¼ inch of olive oil until shimmering. Add the shallot and fry, stirring, until golden and crisp, 1 to 2 minutes. Using a slotted spoon, transfer the shallot to paper towels to drain; season with salt.

4 Spread the sauce on the bread slices, arrange the smoked fish on top and garnish with the crispy shallot, grated horseradish and chopped dill and parsley. Drizzle with olive oil and serve.

MAKE AHEAD *The potato-dill sauce can be refrigerated overnight.*

Balla pays homage to the freshwater fish soups of eastern Europe using American ingredients like sturgeon, collards and hen-of-the-woods mushrooms. He adds a good dose of heat with New Mexican Hatch green chile. "It's the best American chile I've tasted," he says.

FISHERMAN'S STEW WITH GREEN CHILE & COLLARD GREENS

TOTAL *1 hr*   **MAKES** *6 to 8 servings*

2 tablespoons extra-virgin olive oil

2 large onions, thinly sliced

2 fennel bulbs—halved, cored and thinly sliced

1 large leek, white and light green parts only, halved lengthwise and thinly sliced crosswise

3 garlic cloves, thinly sliced

3 serrano chiles, seeded and thinly sliced

2 tablespoons anchovy paste

2 tablespoons Hatch green chile powder (see Note)

½ pound small collard greens, stems discarded and leaves torn into bite-size pieces

1 quart fish stock or bottled clam juice

1 pound Green Zebra tomatoes, sliced ¼ inch thick

6 ounces hen-of-the-woods mushrooms, separated into bite-size pieces

2 pounds skinless sturgeon or halibut fillet, cut into ¾-inch cubes

Kosher salt and freshly ground black pepper

Lemon wedges and crusty bread, for serving

PAIR WITH *Apple-scented, full-bodied Chardonnay: 2011 Scribe*

1 In a large enameled cast-iron casserole, heat the olive oil. Add the onions, fennel, leek, garlic and chiles and cook over moderately low heat, stirring occasionally, until softened but not browned, about 15 minutes.

2 Add the anchovy paste and chile powder to the casserole and cook, stirring, until the anchovy dissolves, about 3 minutes. Stir in the collard greens and cook until just wilted, about 3 minutes. Add the fish stock and 4 cups of water and bring to a boil. Stir in the tomatoes and mushrooms and simmer over moderately low heat until the collards are just tender and the tomatoes start to soften, about 5 minutes. Add the fish and simmer until just cooked through, about 7 minutes; season with salt and pepper. Ladle the stew into bowls and serve with lemon wedges and crusty bread.

NOTE *New Mexican Hatch green chile powder has a bright, floral, fruity flavor. It is available at gourmet markets and hatchnmgreenchile.com.*

"Traditional chicken paprikás *usually has a bright red gravy with a floury texture," Balla says. For his refined version here, Balla omits the flour and instead thickens the sauce with potato and chicken skin, then purees it with sour cream. The result is a silky gravy rich with chicken flavor.*

CHICKEN PAPRIKÁS

ACTIVE *40 min* **TOTAL** *1 hr 15 min* **MAKES** *8 servings*

8 whole chicken legs
Kosher salt and freshly ground
    black pepper
2 tablespoons extra-virgin olive oil
4 slices of thick-cut bacon, cut into
    1-inch pieces
1 large onion, finely chopped
4 garlic cloves, minced
1 serrano chile, seeded and minced
1 baking potato (½ pound), peeled
    and cut into ½-inch pieces
1 tablespoon tomato paste
1 tablespoon light brown sugar
1 bay leaf
¼ teaspoon dried oregano
1 tablespoon sweet Hungarian
    paprika, plus more for garnish
1 quart chicken stock or
    low-sodium broth
2 tablespoons sour cream, plus
    more for garnish
1 tablespoon apple cider vinegar
Chopped dill, for garnish
Buttered egg noodles, for serving

PAIR WITH *Berried Pinot Noir: 2009 Woodenhead Russian River Valley*

1 Preheat the oven to 400°. Cut the excess skin from the chicken legs and reserve. Arrange the chicken legs on a rimmed baking sheet, skin side up, and season with salt and pepper. Roast for about 25 minutes, until well browned.

2 Meanwhile, in a large enameled cast-iron casserole, heat the olive oil. Add the bacon, onion, garlic, serrano chile and the reserved chicken skin; season with a generous pinch each of salt and pepper. Cook over moderate heat, stirring occasionally, until the onion is just starting to brown, 10 to 12 minutes.

3 Add the potato, tomato paste, brown sugar, bay leaf and oregano to the casserole. Stir in the 1 tablespoon of paprika and cook over moderate heat for 7 minutes, stirring occasionally. Add the stock and bring to a simmer. Add the chicken legs and cook over moderately low heat until the chicken is white throughout, about 25 minutes.

4 Transfer the chicken to a platter and tent with foil. Remove and discard the bay leaf, then ladle the stock and vegetables into a blender or food processor. Add the 2 tablespoons of sour cream and the vinegar and puree until smooth; season the sauce with salt and pepper. Pour the sauce over the chicken and garnish with paprika, sour cream and dill. Serve with buttered egg noodles.

This tangy-spicy soup is based on the Slovak Christmas soup called kapustnica. *The beauty of the soup is its simplicity: There's no browning involved; the ingredients just simmer together in one pot. "You can serve the soup over mashed potatoes or cook diced potato into the base," Balla says.*

SMOKED SAUSAGE & SAUERKRAUT SOUP

ACTIVE 15 min   **TOTAL** 1 hr 45 min   **MAKES** 8 servings

- 3 quarts chicken stock or low-sodium broth
- One 25-ounce jar of sauerkraut with brine
- ½ pound shiitake mushrooms, stems discarded and caps sliced
- ½ cup chopped pitted prunes
- 1 medium leek, white and light green parts only, finely diced
- 1 onion, finely diced
- 2 Hungarian wax peppers— halved, seeded and thinly sliced
- 6 garlic cloves, thinly sliced
- 2 serrano chiles, seeded and thinly sliced
- Kosher salt and freshly ground black pepper
- Four 10-ounce duck legs, skin and excess fat removed
- ¾ pound Gyulai sausage, cut crosswise into ¼-inch slices (see Note)
- 4 large tomatoes, diced
- Mashed potatoes, for serving

PAIR WITH Dry, malty English bitter beer: Fuller's ESB

1 In a large pot, combine the stock with the sauerkraut and its brine. Stir in the mushrooms, prunes, leek, onion, wax peppers, garlic, serrano chiles and a generous pinch each of salt and pepper. Add the duck legs and sausage and bring to a boil. Simmer over moderately low heat until the duck is tender, about 1 hour.

2 Remove the soup from the heat and stir in the tomatoes. Cover and let stand until the tomatoes are softened, about 30 minutes. Bring the soup back to a simmer and season with salt and pepper. Serve over mashed potatoes.

NOTE Gyulai, a Hungarian smoked sausage, is available at Hungarian butchers and amazon.com. Spanish chorizo will also work in this recipe.

MAKE AHEAD The soup can be refrigerated for up to 4 days. Reheat gently before serving.

For this elegant, no-bake cheesecake, Balla ferments his own farmer's cheese (a kind of cottage cheese) at Bar Tartine. Ricotta mixed with cream cheese makes a delicious substitute for the filling, which is incredibly light, delicately sweet and wonderful inside the crumbly graham cracker crust.

FARMER'S CHEESECAKE WITH STRAWBERRIES

ACTIVE *40 min*　**TOTAL** *3 hr 15 min*　**MAKES** *8 servings*

CRUST

- 5　tablespoons unsalted butter
- 3　tablespoons sugar
- 1¼　cups packed graham cracker crumbs (10 to 12 whole crackers)
- ¼　teaspoon salt
- Pinch of ground ginger
- Pinch of cinnamon

FILLING

- 1　pound fresh ricotta cheese, at room temperature
- ½　pound cream cheese, at room temperature
- 3　tablespoons agave nectar
- ½　teaspoon finely grated lemon zest
- 1　tablespoon fresh lemon juice
- ¼　teaspoon salt
- Pinch of ground ginger

TOPPINGS

- 1　pint strawberries, hulled and sliced ¼ inch thick
- ¼　cup sugar
- 1　tablespoon fresh lemon juice
- 2　teaspoons caraway seeds
- ½　cup honey

1 MAKE THE CRUST In a small saucepan, melt the butter with the sugar over moderately low heat, stirring, until the sugar dissolves, about 4 minutes. In a medium bowl, mix the graham cracker crumbs with the salt, ginger and cinnamon. Stir in the melted butter until the crumbs are evenly moistened. Press the crumbs evenly over the bottom and up the side of a 9-inch fluted tart pan. Cover with plastic wrap and refrigerate until well chilled, about 1 hour.

2 MAKE THE FILLING In a large bowl, using a handheld electric mixer, beat the ricotta with the cream cheese, agave nectar, lemon zest, lemon juice, salt and ginger just until smooth. Using a spatula, spread the filling in the chilled crust. Cover with plastic wrap and refrigerate until well chilled, about 2 hours.

3 MEANWHILE, PREPARE THE TOPPINGS In a medium bowl, toss the strawberries with the sugar and lemon juice. Let stand at room temperature, stirring once or twice, until the berries are juicy and slightly softened, about 30 minutes.

4 In a small saucepan, toast the caraway seeds over moderate heat until fragrant, about 1 minute. Transfer to a mortar and lightly crush the seeds. Return the caraway seeds to the saucepan and add the honey. Warm the honey over moderately low heat for 10 minutes. Strain the honey into a bowl, discarding the seeds; let cool.

5 Cut the cheesecake into wedges, top with the strawberries and caraway honey and serve.

MAKE AHEAD *The cheesecake can be refrigerated for up to 2 days. The honey can be stored in an airtight container at room temperature for up to 1 month.*

JIMMY BANNOS, JR

CHEF / CO-OWNER • THE PURPLE PIG • CHICAGO

a meat geek with a penchant for pork, Jimmy Bannos, Jr., is one of the country's most audacious nose-to-tail specialists. At the Purple Pig, he gets a kick out of introducing diners to squirm-inducing pig parts, turning them into playful, delicious, Mediterranean-inflected dishes. He rubs pig's tails with brown sugar and then braises them in balsamic vinegar; he combines pig's ears with crispy kale and pickled peppers to make his signature salad. "Jimmy doesn't follow trends, he sets them," says his father, famed Chicago chef-restaurateur Jimmy Bannos, Sr., of the Cajun-inspired Heaven on Seven. "With his pig's ears dish I thought, *Really?* But people go crazy for them. He sometimes sells a hundred orders a night."

Jimmy Bannos, Jr., is the fourth generation of his family to enter the restaurant business. "I've got to believe that cooking is in my DNA," he says. At the age of three he was helping set out condiments for diners and following his dad to the market, eventually working in the kitchen at Heaven on Seven when he was tall enough to reach the counter.

Initially Bannos shared his father's interest in Cajun food, but a stint in the northern Italian kitchen at Al Forno in Providence led him to apprentice in Tuscany. He had spent three-plus years exploring regional Italian food with Mario Batali in New York City when his father asked him to return to Chicago to be the chef of a new restaurant he was opening. "I was terrified. I was 24 years old and had never run a kitchen or created a menu," Bannos says. "But I thought, What the hell, I'll give it a shot." So he moved home in 2009 and opened the Purple Pig later that year with his father and local chefs Scott Harris of Mia Francesca and Tony Mantuano of Spiaggia as partners.

To create the Purple Pig menu, Bannos drew on all his culinary training as well as his own Italian and Greek heritage, revamping dishes he grew up eating. For instance, his ziti with pork gravy and ricotta (page 48) is a more refined version of the pasta with pork neck-bone sauce his Italian grandmother served at Sunday suppers. Grilled lamb chops are a nod to the Greek ancestry on his father's side. He uses brined grape leaves to create a tangy salsa verde and serves the lamb with quinoa tossed with typical Greek salad ingredients (page 56). Most chefs make osso buco with veal, but Bannos's version features pork shanks slow-braised in a tomato sauce ramped up with anchovies and crushed red pepper (page 52). "The fat just melts in your mouth," he says.

For a pork aficionado, Bannos shows surprising deftness with vegetables. For example, he chars cauliflower florets on the *plancha* (a Spanish flat-top grill—another one of his obsessions), giving them a wonderful smokiness, then adds fresh parsley leaves, vinegary cornichons and crisp, toasted bread crumbs (page 40). "I take vegetables just as seriously as meat," he says. "Appreciating them is cultural: Italians and Greeks, we love our vegetables."

As the son of a big-name chef, Bannos could have easily coasted in his career, but that's not his style. "People were hard on me because of my family connections," he says. "I knew I couldn't deck these guys. Instead, I used it as motivation to work even harder in the kitchen." That experience has given him the toughness to match his cooking ability. "He's a young, bright talent making a real name for himself now," says *Chicago Tribune* restaurant critic Phil Vettel. "It's nice to see a new Bannos generation feeding Chicago."

35

> " I take vegetables just as seriously as meat. It's cultural: Italians and Greeks, we love our vegetables. Even vegetarians can come to the Purple Pig and enjoy themselves.

LUNCH • DINNER • LATE NIGHT

Bannos gives this simple salad a great, satisfying crunch with romaine lettuce, watermelon radishes and ciabatta croutons. He whisks sparkling water into the vinaigrette to help mellow the tang of the red wine vinegar.

ROMAINE & ARUGULA SALAD WITH RADISHES, MINT & FETA

TOTAL *30 min*   **MAKES** *6 servings*

½ pound ciabatta, cut into ½-inch cubes

¼ cup plus 2 tablespoons extra-virgin olive oil

Kosher salt and freshly ground black pepper

¼ cup red wine vinegar

2 tablespoons sparkling water

1 romaine lettuce heart (1 pound), cut crosswise into ½-inch strips

5 ounces baby arugula

6 medium watermelon radishes— peeled, halved and thinly sliced

¼ cup finely chopped mint

4 ounces feta cheese, crumbled

1 Preheat the oven to 350°. On a rimmed baking sheet, toss the ciabatta cubes with ¼ cup of the olive oil and season with salt and pepper. Spread the cubes in an even layer and bake for 15 minutes, tossing once, until golden and crisp. Let the croutons cool completely.

2 In a small bowl, whisk the vinegar with the sparkling water and the remaining 2 tablespoons of olive oil. Season the vinaigrette with salt and pepper.

3 In a large bowl, toss the romaine with the arugula, radishes and mint. Add the vinaigrette and toss to coat. Fold in the croutons and feta and season with salt and pepper. Serve right away.

Stuck with a case of cauliflower in the Purple Pig kitchen during a blizzard, Bannos threw some on the flat-top grill until it was charred and smoky. "I never had cauliflower that way," he says. The next day he put the dish on the menu, adding tart cornichons and toasted bread crumbs.

CHARRED CAULIFLOWER WITH CORNICHONS

TOTAL *45 min*   **MAKES** *6 to 8 servings*

5   ounces day-old Italian bread,
    cut into ½-inch pieces
½   cup extra-virgin olive oil
Kosher salt and freshly ground pepper
2   heads of cauliflower, preferably
    green and white—halved, cored
    and cut into 1-inch florets
1   cup lightly packed parsley leaves
¾   cup thinly sliced cornichons
2   tablespoons fresh lemon juice

1 Preheat the oven to 325°. In a pie plate, toss the bread with 2 tablespoons of the olive oil and season with salt and pepper. Bake for about 15 minutes, until golden and crisp. Transfer the croutons to a food processor and pulse until coarse bread crumbs form.

2 Preheat a grill pan. In a large bowl, toss the cauliflower with 3 tablespoons of the olive oil and season with salt and pepper. Grill half of the florets in the hot pan over moderately high heat, turning, until crisp-tender and charred in spots, 7 to 10 minutes; transfer to a large bowl. Repeat with the remaining cauliflower.

3 Add the parsley, cornichons, lemon juice and the remaining 3 tablespoons of olive oil to the cauliflower and toss well. Season with salt and pepper. Sprinkle the bread crumbs on top and serve.

MAKE AHEAD *The cauliflower can stand at room temperature for up to 4 hours. Sprinkle the bread crumbs on top just before serving.*

Despite its name, the Purple Pig serves fantastic vegetarian dishes like this lovely, light grain salad. Red pearl onions are worth seeking out here; they lend a wonderful sweetness and a beautiful purple hue to the combination of tender peas, creamy feta and nutty, chewy farro.

FARRO SALAD WITH SPRING PEAS, ONIONS & FETA

TOTAL *45 min* **MAKES** *6 servings*

1   pound pearled farro
1½   cups peas, thawed if frozen
½   pound red pearl onions,
      root ends trimmed
¼   cup plus 1 tablespoon extra-
      virgin olive oil
Kosher salt and freshly ground pepper
¼   cup fresh lemon juice
½   cup crumbled feta cheese
½   cup chopped mint
1½   teaspoons finely chopped oregano

1 In a large saucepan, cover the farro with 2 inches of water. Bring to a boil and simmer over moderately low heat until the farro is al dente, about 25 minutes. Drain the farro and spread it out on a baking sheet to cool completely.

2 Meanwhile, in a medium saucepan of salted boiling water, cook the peas until tender, 3 to 5 minutes. Using a slotted spoon, transfer the peas to a sieve and cool under running water. Add the onions to the saucepan and blanch just until the skins start to wrinkle, 1 to 2 minutes. Drain the onions and cool them under running water, then peel them.

3 Preheat a grill pan. In a large bowl, toss the onions with 1 tablespoon of the olive oil and season with salt and pepper. Grill the onions over moderately high heat, tossing occasionally, until they are softened and charred in spots, about 8 minutes. Return the onions to the bowl and let them cool. Add the cooled farro, peas, lemon juice and the remaining ¼ cup of olive oil. Fold in the feta, mint and oregano, season the salad with salt and pepper and serve.

MAKE AHEAD *The farro salad can be refrigerated overnight. Fold in the feta, mint and oregano just before serving.*

Bannos improves on the classic BLT by layering his version with curly frisée, lemony arugula aioli, thick-cut bacon and juicy heirloom tomatoes. He tops it all with a runny fried egg.

FRIED-EGG BLTS WITH ARUGULA AIOLI

TOTAL *45 min* **MAKES** *6 servings*

1 tablespoon pine nuts
1½ cups lightly packed baby arugula
   (2 ounces)
¼ cup lightly packed parsley leaves
¼ cup lightly packed basil leaves
1 garlic clove
1 cup mayonnaise
2 tablespoons freshly grated
   Parmigiano-Reggiano cheese
¼ cup extra-virgin olive oil,
   plus more for brushing
1½ tablespoons fresh lemon juice
Kosher salt and freshly ground pepper
12 thick-cut slices of rustic
   Italian bread
12 slices of thick-cut bacon
   (12 ounces)
2 large heirloom tomatoes, sliced
   ¼ inch thick
3 ounces frisée, torn into
   bite-size pieces (1½ cups)
6 large eggs

PAIR WITH *Juicy, full-bodied Italian rosé: 2011 Cantalupo il Mimo*

1 In a small skillet, toast the pine nuts over moderate heat until lightly golden, about 4 minutes. Let cool.

2 In a food processor, combine the pine nuts, arugula, parsley, basil and garlic and pulse until coarsely chopped. Add the mayonnaise, grated cheese, 1 tablespoon of the olive oil and 1 tablespoon of the lemon juice and puree until smooth. Season the aioli with salt and pepper.

3 Preheat a large griddle. Brush both sides of the bread slices with olive oil and griddle over moderate heat, turning once, until toasted, about 2 minutes. Transfer the toasts to a plate. Add the bacon to the griddle and cook over moderate heat until crisp, 3 to 4 minutes per side; drain on paper towels.

4 In a medium bowl, gently toss the tomato slices and torn frisée with 1 tablespoon of the olive oil and the remaining ½ tablespoon of lemon juice; season with salt and pepper.

5 In a large nonstick skillet, heat the remaining 2 tablespoons of oil. Crack the eggs into the skillet and fry sunny-side up or over-easy. Transfer to a plate and season with salt and pepper.

6 Lay 6 slices of toast on a work surface and spread with the aioli. Top with the tomatoes and frisée, then the bacon and eggs. Close the sandwiches, cut in half and serve right away.

For his take on chicken souvlaki (Greek skewers of grilled meat), Bannos sears marinated chicken thighs on a cast-iron griddle, which gives them "the crispiest, best skin ever," he says. To serve alongside the skewers, he fries smashed baby potatoes until they're tender and golden.

CHICKEN KEBABS WITH FRIED SMASHED POTATOES & TZATZIKI

ACTIVE *1 hr 15 min*   **TOTAL** *2 hr 45 min*   **MAKES** *4 servings*

CHICKEN

    2 pounds boneless chicken thighs
       with skin, cut into 1-inch pieces
    ¼ cup extra-virgin olive oil
    4 garlic cloves, minced
    2 tablespoons paprika
    1 tablespoon Aleppo pepper
       (see Note)
    Kosher salt and freshly ground
       black pepper

TZATZIKI

    1 cup plain whole-milk
       Greek yogurt
    2 tablespoons crème fraîche
    1 tablespoon fresh lemon juice
    1 tablespoon extra-virgin olive oil
    1 garlic clove, minced
    1 teaspoon red wine vinegar
    1 English cucumber—peeled,
       halved lengthwise, seeded and
       finely diced
    2 radishes, finely diced
    Kosher salt and freshly ground pepper

POTATOES

    1 pound baby Yukon Gold potatoes
    Kosher salt
    Vegetable oil, for frying
    Freshly ground pepper

PAIR WITH *Lively, lemony Greek white: 2011 Gaia Thalassitis Assyrtiko*

1 PREPARE THE CHICKEN In a baking dish, toss the chicken with the olive oil, garlic, paprika and Aleppo pepper until well coated. Cover and refrigerate for at least 2 hours or overnight.

2 MAKE THE TZATZIKI In a medium bowl, whisk the yogurt with the crème fraîche, lemon juice, olive oil, garlic and vinegar. Fold in the cucumber and radishes and season with salt and pepper. Cover and refrigerate the tzatziki until well chilled, about 1 hour.

3 MEANWHILE, PREPARE THE POTATOES In a medium saucepan, cover the potatoes with water and bring to a boil. Add a generous pinch of salt and simmer over moderate heat until the potatoes are tender but not falling apart, about 15 minutes. Drain and transfer to a baking sheet to cool completely. Using your hand, gently smash the potatoes into ½-inch-thick rounds.

4 In a large, deep skillet, heat ¼ inch of vegetable oil until shimmering. Add the potatoes and fry over moderately high heat, turning once, until golden and crisp, 7 to 10 minutes. Transfer to paper towels to drain. Season with salt and pepper and keep warm.

5 Preheat the oven to 400°. Preheat a cast-iron griddle. Thread the chicken skin side up onto 12 skewers (see Note) and season with salt and black pepper. Arrange the chicken skewers skin side down on the griddle and cook over moderately high heat until the skin is crisp, about 5 minutes. Transfer the skewers to a baking sheet and roast in the oven for 10 to 12 minutes, until the chicken is cooked through. Serve the kebabs with the crispy potatoes and tzatziki.

NOTE *Aleppo pepper is a moderately hot crushed dried chile from Turkey and Syria; it is available at gourmet markets and penzeys.com. If using bamboo skewers, soak them in water for at least 30 minutes before threading.*

MAKE AHEAD *The tzatziki can be refrigerated overnight.*

Bannos's Italian grandmother served meatballs and sausage along with the pork neck bones in her Sunday-supper gravy. For his version, Bannos picks all the meat off the bones, then stirs it back into the gravy.

ZITI WITH PORK GRAVY & FRESH RICOTTA

ACTIVE *45 min* **TOTAL** *2 hr 30 min* **MAKES** *8 servings*

2½ pounds meaty pork neck bones
Kosher salt and freshly ground pepper
3 tablespoons extra-virgin olive oil
1 large onion, finely chopped
3 garlic cloves, finely chopped
One 14-ounce can crushed tomatoes
One 14-ounce can diced tomatoes
¼ cup finely chopped parsley
¼ cup finely chopped basil
1 tablespoon dried oregano
1 tablespoon dried basil
8 ounces fresh ricotta cheese
1 pound ziti

PAIR WITH *Earthy, cherry-rich Chianti Classico: 2009 Badia a Coltibuono*

1 Season the pork bones with salt and pepper. In a large enameled cast-iron casserole, heat 2 tablespoons of the olive oil. Add the pork bones and cook over moderately high heat, turning, until they are browned all over, about 8 minutes. Transfer the bones to a plate.

2 Add the onion and garlic to the casserole and cook over moderately high heat until softened, about 8 minutes. Stir in the crushed and diced tomatoes, 1 cup of water and the fresh and dried herbs and bring to a simmer. Return the pork bones to the casserole and simmer over low heat until the meat is very tender, about 2 hours. Using a slotted spoon, transfer the bones to a plate and let cool slightly. Pick the meat from the bones and stir it into the gravy. Season the pork gravy with salt and pepper and keep warm.

3 In a small bowl, whisk the ricotta with the remaining 1 tablespoon of olive oil and season with salt and pepper.

4 In a large pot of salted boiling water, cook the ziti until al dente. Drain and return to the pot. Stir the pork gravy into the pasta and season with salt and pepper. Spoon the pasta into bowls, top with the ricotta cheese and serve.

MAKE AHEAD *The pork gravy can be refrigerated for up to 3 days. Reheat gently before proceeding.*

Braising pork in milk, a method that Bannos learned while cooking in Florence, results in supertender meat and an incredibly rich and flavorful gravy. Although the dish is rooted in Tuscan tradition, Bannos adds an American comfort-food spin by serving it with mashed potatoes.

MILK-BRAISED PORK CHOPS WITH MASHED POTATOES & GRAVY

ACTIVE *1 hr 10 min* **TOTAL** *3 hr* **MAKES** *6 servings*

2 tablespoons extra-virgin olive oil
Six 8-ounce well-marbled boneless
    pork loin chops
Kosher salt and freshly ground pepper
1 large onion, chopped
1 large carrot, chopped
2 celery ribs, chopped
5 garlic cloves, smashed
2 cups chicken stock
    or low-sodium broth
5 thyme sprigs
5 bay leaves
2½ cups whole milk
3 pounds baking potatoes, peeled
    and cut into 1-inch pieces
1 cup heavy cream
6 tablespoons unsalted butter
2 tablespoons all-purpose flour

PAIR WITH *Bright, medium-bodied Barbera d'Alba: 2010 Sottimano Pairolero*

1 In a large enameled cast-iron casserole, heat the olive oil until shimmering. Season the pork chops with salt and pepper and add them to the casserole. Cook over moderately high heat, turning once, until golden, about 7 minutes total. Transfer the pork chops to a plate.

2 Add the onion, carrot, celery, garlic and a generous pinch each of salt and pepper to the casserole and cook over moderately high heat, stirring, until the vegetables just start to soften, about 5 minutes. Add the stock, thyme, bay leaves and 2 cups of the milk and bring to a simmer. Return the pork chops to the casserole, cover and braise over very low heat until tender, about 2 hours.

3 Meanwhile, in a large saucepan, cover the potatoes with water and bring to a boil. Add a generous pinch of salt and simmer over moderate heat until the potatoes are tender, about 20 minutes. Drain well. Add the cream and 4 tablespoons of the butter to the saucepan and warm over moderately low heat until the butter is melted. Pass the potatoes through a ricer into a serving bowl, then stir in the warm cream and butter. Season the mashed potatoes with salt and pepper; keep warm.

4 Transfer the pork chops to a platter and cover with foil. Spoon 4 cups of the braising liquid and vegetables into a blender, discarding the bay leaves, thyme sprigs and remaining vegetables and liquid. Puree the sauce until smooth.

5 In a medium saucepan, melt the remaining 2 tablespoons of butter over moderately high heat. Whisk in the flour and cook until bubbling. Whisk in the sauce and the remaining ½ cup of milk; cook over moderate heat, whisking, until the gravy is thickened and no floury taste remains, about 10 minutes. Season with salt and pepper. Serve the pork chops with the mashed potatoes and gravy.

In place of the veal shanks typically used in osso buco, Bannos braises pork shanks with tomatoes and wine. He adds anchovies, crushed red pepper and lemon zest to the braise, creating a complex and deeply flavored sauce that's phenomenal served over creamy polenta.

PORK SHANK OSSO BUCO

ACTIVE *1 hr*   **TOTAL** *4 hr plus overnight salting*   **MAKES** *6 to 8 servings*

6 pork shanks (7½ pounds;
     see Note)
Kosher salt and freshly ground
     black pepper
3 tablespoons extra-virgin olive oil
1 large white onion, chopped
1 large carrot, chopped
1 celery rib, chopped
3 garlic cloves, minced
2 anchovy fillets, minced
1 tablespoon finely grated
     lemon zest
½ teaspoon crushed red pepper
1 cup dry white wine
Two 28-ounce cans crushed tomatoes
2 cups chicken stock
     or low-sodium broth
5 thyme sprigs
2 rosemary sprigs
2 bay leaves
Creamy polenta, for serving

PAIR WITH *Lively, medium-bodied Montepulciano: 2009 Fattoria Le Terrazze Rosso Conero*

1 In a baking dish, season the pork shanks with salt and black pepper. Cover and refrigerate overnight.

2 Preheat the oven to 325°. In a large enameled cast-iron casserole, heat the olive oil until shimmering. Add 3 of the shanks in a single layer and cook over moderately high heat, turning occasionally, until browned, about 8 minutes. Transfer the shanks to a large roasting pan. Repeat with the remaining 3 shanks.

3 Pour off all but 2 tablespoons of the fat from the casserole. Add the onion, carrot, celery and a generous pinch each of salt and black pepper and cook over moderately high heat, stirring occasionally, until the vegetables are softened and just starting to brown, about 10 minutes. Stir in the garlic, anchovies, lemon zest and crushed red pepper and cook until fragrant. Add the wine and simmer until reduced by half, about 3 minutes. Add the tomatoes, stock, thyme, rosemary and bay leaves and bring to a boil. Pour the mixture over the shanks in the roasting pan. Cover tightly with foil and braise in the oven for about 3 hours, until the meat is very tender.

4 Transfer the pork shanks to a platter and tent with foil. Discard the herbs and spoon off the fat from the sauce. Working in batches, puree the sauce in a blender until smooth. Season with salt and black pepper. Spoon some of the sauce over the pork shanks and pass the remaining sauce at the table. Serve the osso buco with creamy polenta.

NOTE *Pork shanks are available at some supermarkets and dartagnan.com.*

MAKE AHEAD *The pork shanks can be refrigerated in the sauce for up to 2 days. Reheat gently before serving.*

Asked why he uses pork in his saltimbocca (a Roman dish prepared with veal, prosciutto and sage), Bannos responds, "Because pork is better." When he fries the pork, he uses a spatula to press the prosciutto into the chops until it's like a crust, a technique he learned cooking at Lupa in Manhattan.

PORK SALTIMBOCCA

TOTAL *1 hr*　**MAKES** *6 servings*

2½ pounds Swiss chard—stemmed, leaves cut into 2-inch pieces, ½ cup diced stems reserved
1 stick unsalted butter
¼ cup fresh lemon juice
Kosher salt and freshly ground black pepper
Twelve 3-ounce boneless pork loin chops, pounded ¼ inch thick
12 thin slices of prosciutto di Parma
12 sage leaves
Wondra flour, for dusting (see Note)
⅓ cup extra-virgin olive oil
2 garlic cloves, thinly sliced
½ teaspoon crushed red pepper

PAIR WITH *Juicy, fruity Dolcetto: 2010 Elio Altare*

1 In a large pot of salted boiling water, blanch the Swiss chard leaves and stems for 1 minute. Drain and cool under running water. Drain well and pat dry.

2 In a small saucepan, melt the butter over moderately low heat. Whisk in the lemon juice and season with salt and black pepper; keep warm.

3 Season the pork with salt and black pepper. Place 1 slice of prosciutto on each chop, folding the slices to fit. Press the sage leaves onto the prosciutto, then dust the pork with Wondra flour.

4 In a very large skillet, heat the olive oil until shimmering. Carefully add half of the pork, prosciutto side down, and press with a spatula. Cook over high heat until golden on the bottom, about 2 minutes. Flip the pork and cook until barely pink throughout, about 1 minute longer. Transfer the saltimbocca to a serving platter and tent with foil. Repeat with the remaining pork chops.

5 Pour off all but 2 tablespoons of the oil from the skillet. Add the garlic and crushed red pepper and cook over moderate heat until fragrant, 1 minute. Add the Swiss chard and cook, tossing, until heated through. Season with salt and black pepper. Transfer the Swiss chard to plates and top with the saltimbocca. Drizzle the lemon butter over the meat and serve right away.

NOTE *Wondra flour, also known as instant flour, is more granular than regular flour and dissolves quickly, making it ideal for thickening sauces and gravies. It also becomes a silky coating for ingredients like the pork here. It's available at most supermarkets.*

Bannos pays homage to his Greek heritage with this lamb dish. He combines brined grape leaves—traditionally stuffed with rice—with capers and herbs to create a tangy condiment for the lamb, then tosses quinoa with classic Greek salad components for a superhealthy and tasty side.

LAMB CHOPS WITH GRAPE LEAF SALSA VERDE

TOTAL *1 hr 30 min plus 6 hr marinating*   **MAKES** *4 servings*

MARINATED LAMB
½ cup extra-virgin olive oil
5 garlic cloves, chopped
3 anchovy fillets, chopped
1 tablespoon finely chopped rosemary
1 teaspoon finely chopped oregano
½ teaspoon crushed red pepper
Four 10-ounce lamb loin chops
Kosher salt and freshly ground black pepper

SALSA VERDE
½ cup chopped jarred grape leaves
2 garlic cloves
1 tablespoon capers, rinsed
1 anchovy fillet
2 tablespoons chopped parsley
1 teaspoon chopped oregano
½ teaspoon chopped rosemary
½ cup extra-virgin olive oil
1 tablespoon fresh lemon juice
Kosher salt and freshly ground pepper

SALAD
1 cup quinoa
Kosher salt and freshly ground pepper
½ cup finely diced cucumber
½ cup pitted kalamata olives
½ small red onion, thinly sliced
¼ cup finely diced oil-packed sun-dried tomatoes
2 tablespoons each finely chopped parsley and mint
1   tablespoon red wine vinegar
1 tablespoon fresh lemon juice
2 tablespoons extra-virgin olive oil

PAIR WITH *Minerally, cherry-scented Greek red: 2008 Kir-Yianni Ramnista Xinomavro*

1 MARINATE THE LAMB In a small saucepan, combine the olive oil, garlic, anchovies, rosemary, oregano and crushed red pepper. Warm over moderately low heat until the anchovies have dissolved and the herbs are fragrant, about 10 minutes. Let the marinade cool completely, then transfer to a resealable plastic bag; add the lamb chops and turn to coat. Refrigerate for at least 6 hours or overnight. Let the lamb chops come to room temperature before grilling.

2 MAKE THE SALSA VERDE In the bowl of a food processor, pulse the grape leaves with the garlic, capers, anchovy fillet, parsley, oregano and rosemary until finely chopped. Add the olive oil and lemon juice; pulse until blended. Season the salsa verde with salt and pepper and transfer to a small bowl.

3 MAKE THE SALAD In a medium saucepan, combine the quinoa with 2 cups of water and a generous pinch of salt and bring to a boil. Cover and simmer until the quinoa is tender and the water is absorbed, about 18 minutes. Remove from the heat and let stand for 5 minutes; uncover and let cool. Transfer the quinoa to a medium bowl and add the cucumber, olives, onion, sun-dried tomatoes, parsley, mint, vinegar, lemon juice and olive oil; toss well. Season the quinoa salad with salt and pepper.

4 Light a grill. Remove the lamb chops from the marinade and season with salt and black pepper. Grill over moderate heat, turning once, until the lamb is lightly charred, about 10 minutes. Close the grill and cook over moderately low heat until the lamb is medium-rare, 7 to 10 minutes longer. Transfer the lamb to plates and let rest for 5 minutes. Top with the grape leaf salsa verde and serve the quinoa salad alongside.

MAKE AHEAD *The grape leaf salsa verde and quinoa salad can be refrigerated separately for up to 6 hours.*

JULIANNE JONES + DIDIER MURAT

OWNERS • VERGENNES LAUNDRY • VERGENNES, VERMONT

the artisanal and digital

collide at Vergennes Laundry, a bakery in Vermont's smallest, oldest city. Judging from the menu, the place could be something out of 19th-century Paris: Extraordinary baguettes, *sablés* (shortbread cookies) and croissants all emerge from the hand-built, wood-fired brick oven. That oven, however, exists only because of $12,000 from Kickstarter.com, a crowd-sourced fundraising site for digital-savvy entrepreneurs. And the woman who designed and uses that oven, Julianne Jones, is a self-taught 27-year-old who learned to make impeccable *macarons* from food blogs.

Jones and her husband, French-born Didier Murat, have put together a bakery that could only exist now: run by first-timers, funded by strangers and deeply dedicated to a challenging craft, artisanal French baking. Jones was studying to be an architect at Vermont's Middlebury College when she detoured into baking, working at Christophe's on the Green, a French restaurant in nearby Vergennes. Christophe Lissarrague, the former chef-owner, used to tease her: "Don't you have more interesting things to do than come here and plate desserts?" Today he recalls, "She told me the best part of her day was working at the restaurant." Around the same time, Jones met Murat, and baking became part of their courtship. "I started by making *macarons* for Didier, even though I never had a *macaron* until I made one," recalls Jones. "Didier loved them."

Not long after, Jones contacted Vermont bread baker Gérard Rubaud, a recluse reachable only via snail mail. What she saw amazed her. With laserlike focus, Rubaud made only one kind of bread, a blend of rye, spelt and wheat flours leavened with a natural starter. She became his apprentice. "I loved being immersed in

his early mornings," she says. "We listened to French radio. The smell of the fire, the music, the atmosphere—it was a beautiful thing." The care she once took in building architectural models translated into a meticulousness about making and shaping dough.

After three months, Jones returned to Vergennes with a vision for a bakery, one tightly focused on natural yeasts, slow-rising breads and super-traditional French pastries. She and Murat found a former laundromat on Vergennes's Main Street and designed a bright, white space where, she says, "If I had to be there 18 hours a day, I'd still be happy."

When the wood fire is at full blast, Jones bakes her crusty loaves and baguettes for the bakery's lunch sandwiches, like asparagus with aged goat cheese (page 68), and the flaky shells for her savory tarts. She uses the same *levain* dough to make an inventive *tarte flambée* (page 66). Instead of topping the Alsatian-style flatbread with bacon and onions, Jones layers on potatoes, rosemary and crème fraîche, highlighting the tang of the sourdough base. On days the bakery is closed, she uses the oven's residual heat to bake crisp, buttery French-style hazelnut-fig biscotti (page 76), which she jokes have become "the official teething biscuits of Vergennes." Murat, a confectioner, contributes another chewy sweet to the menu: almond-and-pistachio-packed nougat (page 80).

Despite many requests, Jones doesn't offer American-style pastries like muffins or cupcakes. Instead, she sticks with French classics like *macarons*, croissants and tricky *cannelés*, small pastries with a caramelized crust and a soft custard center. "I love that kids come in to get a *cannelé*," she says. "It's fun to think Vermonters are growing up with this memory."

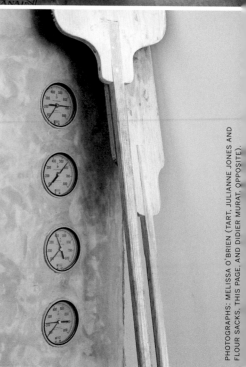

> **Jones and Murat have put together a bakery that could only exist now: run by first-timers, funded by strangers and deeply dedicated to time-consuming artisanal French baking.**

```
GREEN TART   $3.75

asparagus, wild foraged ramps
and fiddleheads, meyer lemon
zest, creme fraiche,
pecorino romano,
pain au levain crust
```

Pears and parsnips create an unusual sweet-savory topping for Jones's French-style open-face sandwiches called tartines. *Toasted briefly under the broiler, the* tartines *are best eaten hot, while the parsnips are still crisp and the Fourme d'Ambert (a mild blue cheese) is gooey.*

PEAR, PARSNIP & FOURME D'AMBERT TARTINES

ACTIVE *25 min*　**TOTAL** *50 min*　**MAKES** *4 servings*

- 2　medium parsnips, thinly shaved lengthwise on a mandoline or with a vegetable peeler
- 1　tablespoon extra-virgin olive oil
- Salt and freshly ground pepper
- Four ¾-inch-thick slices of sourdough bread or eight ¾-inch-thick slices of baguette cut on the diagonal
- ¼　cup crème fraîche
- 1　Bosc pear—halved, cored and thinly sliced lengthwise
- 4　ounces Fourme d'Ambert, rind removed, cheese thinly sliced

PAIR WITH *Sparkling rosé: NV Lucien Albrecht Crémant d'Alsace Brut Rosé*

1 Preheat the oven to 350°. On a rimmed baking sheet, toss the parsnips with the olive oil and season with salt and pepper. Roast for about 20 minutes, tossing once, until the parsnips are tender and starting to crisp around the edges. Let cool slightly.

2 Preheat the broiler. Arrange the bread slices on a baking sheet. Spread equal amounts of the crème fraîche on each, then top with the pear slices, parsnips and cheese; season with salt and pepper. Broil 8 inches from the heat for about 3 minutes, until the cheese is melted. Serve the *tartines* hot.

Jones makes this savory rectangular tart with the ingredients typically found in ratatouille: eggplant, zucchini and tomatoes. "You arrange the vegetables nicely in the flaky crust, then tuck in thinly shaved cheese," she says. "I love serving the tart at dinner parties because it's aesthetically impressive."

PROVENÇAL VEGETABLE TART

ACTIVE *45 min* **TOTAL** *2 hr 30 min* **MAKES** *one 4-by-14-inch tart or two 10-inch round tarts • 6 servings*

TART SHELL

1¾ cups all-purpose flour, plus more
    for dusting
½ teaspoon salt
1 stick plus 2 tablespoons
   cold unsalted butter, cubed
¼ cup ice water

FILLING

3½ tablespoons extra-virgin olive oil,
    plus more for drizzling
1 small yellow bell pepper—cored,
   seeded and sliced ¼ inch thick
1 medium onion,
   cut into ¼-inch wedges
Salt and freshly ground black pepper
1 small Japanese eggplant,
   sliced ¼ inch thick
1 small zucchini, sliced ¼ inch thick
½ cup grape tomatoes
2 teaspoons Champagne vinegar
1 teaspoon fresh thyme leaves
1 teaspoon chopped basil
2 ounces thinly sliced Tomme de
   Savoie or imported Fontina cheese

PAIR WITH *Bright, light-bodied red: 2010 Potel-Aviron Morgon Côte du Py*

1 **MAKE THE TART SHELL** In a food processor, combine the 1¾ cups of flour with the salt. Add the butter cubes and pulse 5 times in 1-second bursts. Add the ice water and pulse until the dough comes together, then turn the dough out onto a floured work surface and knead briefly. Flatten the dough into a disk, wrap in plastic and refrigerate for about 30 minutes, until firm.

2 Preheat the oven to 375°. On a floured work surface, roll out the dough to a 6-by-16-inch rectangle, a scant ¼ inch thick. Ease the pastry into a 4-by-14-inch tart mold and trim the overhang to ½ inch. Fold the overhang over to reinforce the edges. Freeze the tart shell for about 15 minutes, until firm.

3 Line the tart shell with parchment paper and pie weights and bake in the center of the oven for 35 minutes, until set. Remove the parchment and weights and bake for about 10 minutes longer, until golden. Let cool.

4 **MEANWHILE, MAKE THE FILLING** Drizzle a baking sheet with olive oil. In a bowl, toss the bell pepper and onion with ½ tablespoon of the oil, season with salt and pepper and arrange on one-quarter of the baking sheet. Add the eggplant to the

bowl, toss with ½ tablespoon of the oil, season with salt and pepper and arrange on another quarter of the baking sheet. Repeat with the zucchini and tomatoes, using ½ tablespoon of oil for each.

5 Roast the vegetables for about 45 minutes, turning once, until tender. Let cool slightly, then return them to the bowl. Add the vinegar, herbs and the remaining 1½ tablespoons of oil and toss; season with salt and pepper.

6 Arrange the vegetables in the tart shell, tuck in the cheese slices and serve.

For her spectacular vegetarian take on tarte flambée *(Alsatian-style pizza with onions and bacon), Jones layers thin potato slices on French sourdough* (levain), *adding crème fraîche for extra tanginess. The key to achieving a crisp crust is stretching the dough thin and baking it quickly in a very hot oven.*

POTATO TARTE FLAMBÉE

ACTIVE *45 min*   **TOTAL** *1 hr 50 min*   **MAKES** *4 to 6 servings*

All-purpose flour, for dusting

Two 6-ounce balls of levain *dough (sourdough; see Note)*

Extra-virgin olive oil, for brushing and drizzling

¼ cup crème fraîche

¼ pound Red Norland or other red potatoes, sliced crosswise ⅟₁₆ inch thick on a mandoline

¼ cup lightly packed rosemary leaves

2 teaspoons finely grated lemon zest, preferably Meyer lemon

Maldon sea salt (see Note) and freshly ground black pepper

PAIR WITH *Ripe, full-bodied Alsace white: 2010 Domaines Schlumberger Les Princes Abbés Pinot Blanc*

1 On a lightly floured work surface, roll or stretch each piece of *levain* dough to a 6-by-12-inch rectangle. Lightly brush the dough with olive oil, cover it loosely with plastic wrap and let stand at room temperature until slightly puffed, about 45 minutes.

2 Meanwhile, put a pizza stone on the bottom of the oven and preheat the oven to 500°, allowing at least 30 minutes for the stone to preheat.

3 Work with 1 dough rectangle at a time. If the dough has shrunk, gently stretch it to a 6-by-12-inch rectangle and transfer it to a floured pizza peel. Spread 2 tablespoons of the crème fraîche on the dough and arrange half of the potato slices on top, overlapping them slightly. Sprinkle half of the rosemary and lemon zest over the potatoes and drizzle with 1 tablespoon of olive oil. Season with Maldon sea salt and black pepper.

4 Slide the rectangle onto the hot pizza stone and bake for 8 to 10 minutes, until golden brown and crisp. Slide the *tarte flambée* onto a work surface, cut into 2-inch strips and serve. Repeat with the remaining dough and toppings.

NOTE *You can buy raw* levain *dough from select bakeries. Maldon sea salt has a great crunch and a remarkably subtle, briny flavor; it is available at most grocery stores and online.*

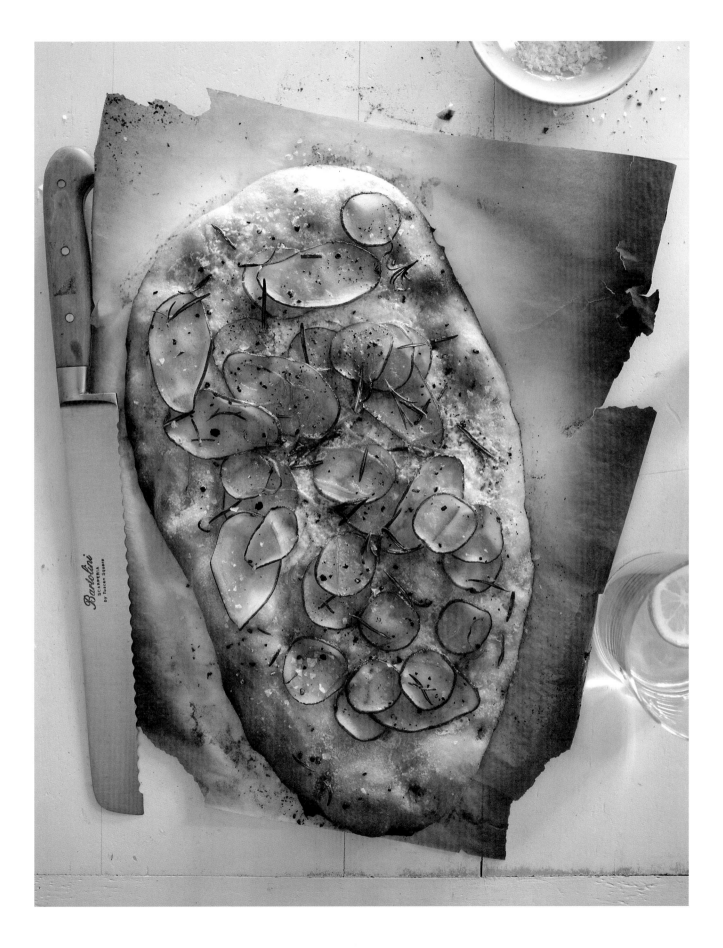

For these terrific sandwiches, Jones uses asparagus both raw (shaved into long, thin strips) and roasted. What also makes these sandwiches distinct is aged goat cheese (not fresh), which adds a richer flavor.

ASPARAGUS & AGED GOAT CHEESE SANDWICHES

TOTAL *30 min*   **MAKES** *4 servings*

1   pound asparagus
1½ tablespoons plus 2 teaspoons extra-virgin olive oil
Salt and freshly ground pepper
2   teaspoons fresh lemon juice
1   cup lightly packed mesclun
½   cup lightly packed mint leaves
2   teaspoons red wine vinegar
4   ounces aged goat cheese, rind removed, cheese shaved
1   Hass avocado—halved, pitted and thinly sliced
Four split 6-inch lengths of baguette, toasted (optional)

1 Preheat the oven to 400°. On a baking sheet, toss half of the asparagus with 2 teaspoons of the olive oil and season with salt and pepper. Roast for 10 to 12 minutes, until tender and charred in spots. Let the asparagus cool.

2 Meanwhile, using a vegetable peeler, shave the remaining asparagus into long, thin strips. In a medium bowl, toss the shaved asparagus with the lemon juice and season with salt and pepper. In another medium bowl, toss the mesclun and mint with the red wine vinegar and the remaining 1½ tablespoons of olive oil; season with salt and pepper.

3 Mound the roasted asparagus, goat cheese, shaved asparagus, mesclun mix and avocado on the baguettes and serve the sandwiches right away.

Jones makes this lovely, luscious soup simply by pureeing celeriac (celery root) with celery and vegetable stock—there's no cream. For an equally delightful chilled version, Jones recommends thinning the soup with a little more stock.

CELERIAC SOUP

ACTIVE *30 min* **TOTAL** *1 hr* **MAKES** *8 to 10 servings*

2 tablespoons extra-virgin olive oil
4 large shallots, minced
Salt
3 pounds celeriac (celery root), peeled and cut into ½-inch pieces
4 celery ribs, cut into ½-inch pieces
6 cups vegetable stock or low-sodium broth
½ lemon
1 tablespoon fresh lemon juice
Celery leaves, for garnish

1 In a large saucepan, heat the olive oil until shimmering. Add the shallots and a generous pinch of salt and cook over moderate heat, stirring, until the shallots are softened and just starting to brown, about 5 minutes. Stir in the celeriac and celery and cook until the celery just starts to soften, about 5 minutes. Add the stock and lemon half, cover and simmer over moderately low heat until the celeriac is tender, about 30 minutes.

2 Remove and discard the lemon half. Working in batches, puree the soup in a blender. Return the soup to the saucepan and warm over low heat. Stir in the lemon juice and season with salt. Ladle the soup into bowls, garnish with celery leaves and serve.

MAKE AHEAD *The soup can be refrigerated overnight. Reheat gently.*

Preparing the parchment packets, or papillotes, is supereasy, says Jones: "Just make the bundles and stick them in the oven." The papillotes puff up with steam as they bake, flavoring the fish with the sorrel, wine and ramps.

SPRING HALIBUT PAPILLOTES WITH SORREL & RAMPS

TOTAL *50 min*   **MAKES** *4 servings*

12 ramps (about 6 ounces; see Note)
1½ pounds skinless halibut fillet,
     cut into 2-inch pieces
 2 tablespoons extra-virgin olive oil
 2 tablespoons snipped chives
Salt and freshly ground pepper
 4 ounces sorrel, cut into 1½-inch
     strips (see Note)
 2 tablespoons plus 2 teaspoons
     crème fraîche
 2 tablespoons plus 2 teaspoons
     dry white wine
 1 teaspoon soy sauce
Crusty bread, for serving

PAIR WITH *Full-bodied, fruity
California Chardonnay: 2011 Wyatt*

1 Preheat the oven to 500°. On a baking sheet, arrange the ramps in a single layer. Roast for 3 to 5 minutes, until the leaves are slightly puffed and beginning to brown at the edges.

2 In a medium bowl, toss the halibut with the olive oil and chives; season with salt and pepper.

3 Lay four 14-inch-long sheets of parchment paper on a work surface. Arrange 3 ramps in the center of each sheet and top with the halibut. Mound the sorrel on the fish and top with the crème fraîche, wine and soy sauce; season with pepper. Fold the parchment over the fish, then fold the edge of the parchment over itself in small pleats to seal the papillotes.

4 Transfer the papillotes to a baking sheet and bake for about 8 to 10 minutes, until they are slightly puffed. Snip the parchment packets open with scissors and serve with crusty bread.

NOTE *If ramps are not available, substitute scallions. If sorrel isn't available, use baby spinach and a squeeze of lemon juice.*

Murat likes to experiment with absinthe. The potent spirit was banned in the United States for nearly 100 years, but, as Murat points out, "It's legal to buy now!" He stirs a little bit of absinthe into the creamy puddings here, giving them a delicate anise flavor.

PETITS POTS À L'ABSINTHE

TOTAL *20 min plus 6 hr chilling*   **MAKES** *6 servings*

1   cup heavy cream
⅔   cup whole milk
2½ tablespoons sugar
1   teaspoon unflavored powdered
    gelatin dissolved in 2 tablespoons
    of water
1½ tablespoons absinthe
Fresh berries, for serving

1 In a medium saucepan, combine the cream with the milk and sugar and bring to a simmer. Off the heat, whisk in the gelatin and absinthe.

2 Strain the mixture through a fine sieve into a pitcher, then pour into six 4-ounce ramekins or bowls. Press a piece of plastic wrap directly onto the surface of the puddings and refrigerate until set, at least 6 hours. Serve with fresh berries.

MAKE AHEAD *The* pots à l'absinthe *can be refrigerated for up to 3 days.*

"The texture of most biscotti can break your teeth," Jones says. So she came up with this softer, chewier version by including butter and sweet dried figs.

BUTTERY HAZELNUT-FIG BISCOTTI

ACTIVE *30 min*   **TOTAL** *2 hr plus cooling*   **MAKES** *about 6 dozen biscotti*

2½ cups hazelnuts (10 ounces)
14 ounces dried Calimyrna figs
1½ sticks cold unsalted butter, cubed
1¾ cups sugar
3 large eggs
3½ cups all-purpose flour
1 tablespoon baking powder
1½ teaspoons salt

1 Preheat the oven to 325° and position racks in the upper and lower thirds of the oven. Spread the hazelnuts on a baking sheet and toast them for 12 to 14 minutes, until the skins blister. Let cool, then transfer the nuts to a clean kitchen towel and rub off as much of the skins as possible. Transfer the nuts to a cutting board and coarsely chop them.

2 Meanwhile, in a microwavable bowl, cover the figs with water and microwave at high power for 1 minute, just until the figs are plumped. Drain well. Trim off the stem ends and slice the figs ⅛ inch thick.

3 In the bowl of a standing mixer fitted with the paddle, beat the butter with the sugar at medium speed until smooth. Beat in the eggs. In a small bowl, whisk the flour with the baking powder and salt. Add the dry ingredients to the butter mixture and beat at low speed until combined. Add the nuts and figs and beat until combined.

4 Line 2 large baking sheets with parchment paper. Transfer the dough to a work surface and roll it into six 10-by-1½-inch logs. Arrange the logs on the lined baking sheets and bake for 30 minutes, or until golden and firm. Let cool for 15 minutes.

5 Transfer the logs to a work surface and, using a serrated knife, cut them on the diagonal into ⅔-inch-thick slices. Arrange the biscotti cut side up on the baking sheets and bake them for about 18 minutes, until lightly browned. Let the biscotti cool, then serve or store.

MAKE AHEAD *The biscotti can be stored in an airtight container at room temperature for up to 2 weeks.*

Jones's wonderfully zingy gingerbread cookies have a tender and cakey texture, yet they're sturdy enough to decorate. As an alternative to the icing here, you can sprinkle the tops of the cookies with demerara sugar (a coarse, raw cane sugar) before baking for a nice crunch.

SPICED GINGERBREAD COOKIES

ACTIVE *45 min*   **TOTAL** *4 hr plus cooling*   **MAKES** *about 2 dozen large cookies*

2¾ cups all-purpose flour, sifted, plus more for dusting
½ teaspoon baking soda
¼ teaspoon baking powder
1 stick unsalted butter, at room temperature
¼ cup plus 1 tablespoon light brown sugar
2 teaspoons ground ginger
1½ teaspoons cinnamon
1 teaspoon Maldon sea salt
¾ teaspoon ground cloves
¾ teaspoon freshly ground black pepper
1 large egg
½ cup unsulfured molasses
1 large egg white
½ pound confectioners' sugar

1 In a medium bowl, whisk the 2¾ cups of flour with the baking soda and baking powder. In the bowl of a standing mixer fitted with the paddle, beat the butter with the brown sugar at medium speed until fluffy, about 2 minutes. Beat in the ginger, cinnamon, salt, cloves and black pepper, then beat in the whole egg. With the mixer on, drizzle in the molasses and beat until blended. Beat in the dry ingredients in 3 batches.

2 Divide the dough in half and pat into disks. Wrap each disk in plastic and refrigerate until well chilled, about 3 hours.

3 Preheat the oven to 325° and line 2 large baking sheets with parchment paper. On a lightly floured work surface, roll out the dough ⅛ inch thick. Using 4- to 5-inch cookie cutters, cut the dough into shapes and transfer to the prepared baking sheets. Reroll the dough scraps and cut out more cookies.

4 Bake the cookies for 8 to 10 minutes, until the tops are dry and the edges just start to darken; rotate the pans halfway through baking. Let the cookies cool on the sheets for 5 minutes, then transfer to racks to cool completely.

5 In a medium bowl, beat the egg white at medium speed until foamy. Add the confectioners' sugar 1 cup at a time, beating between additions, until the sugar is completely incorporated. Add ½ tablespoon of water and beat at high speed until the icing holds its shape, about 5 minutes. Thin with more water as needed.

6 Decorate the cooled cookies with the icing and serve.

MAKE AHEAD *The cookies can be kept in an airtight container at room temperature for up to 5 days.*

Murat makes this soft, chewy nougat at Vergennes Laundry and also sells it under the Vadeboncoeur label online and at specialty food shops. The nougat is fantastic on its own or baked into croissants. "The white part melts away, and it's like honey and nuts," Jones says.

ALMOND-PISTACHIO NOUGAT

ACTIVE *45 min*   **TOTAL** *1 hr plus cooling*   **MAKES** *about 2 pounds*

3 cups roasted almonds
¾ cup unsalted shelled pistachios
¼ cup cornstarch
¼ cup confectioners' sugar
1⅔ cups plus 1 tablespoon
    granulated sugar
¾ cup light honey
2 large egg whites,
    at room temperature
Pinch of salt

1 Preheat the oven to 200°. Spread the almonds and pistachios on a large baking sheet and keep warm in the oven. Line an 8-inch square baking pan with parchment paper, allowing the paper to hang over on 2 opposite sides. Lightly spray the paper with nonstick cooking spray. In a small bowl, combine the cornstarch and confectioners' sugar, then dust the pan with half of the mixture.

2 In a medium saucepan, combine 1⅔ cups of the granulated sugar with ¼ cup of the honey and 1¾ cups of water; bring to a boil. When the syrup reaches 245° on a candy thermometer, after 20 to 30 minutes, bring the remaining ½ cup of honey to a boil in a small saucepan. Continue cooking the sugar syrup.

3 Meanwhile, in the bowl of a standing mixer fitted with the whisk, beat the egg whites with the salt until firm peaks form. Add the remaining 1 tablespoon of granulated sugar; beat until combined.

4 When the pure honey reaches 265° on a candy thermometer, after 5 to 8 minutes, add it in a fast, steady stream to the egg whites with the mixer at medium-high speed. When the sugar syrup reaches 305°, add it to the egg whites in a fast, steady stream and beat at high speed until the mixture is pale, 3 to 5 minutes. Using an oiled wooden spoon, immediately stir in the hot almonds and pistachios (the nougat will be a bit stiff).

5 Scrape the nougat into the prepared pan and, using oiled hands, press it into an even layer. Dust the remaining cornstarch mixture on top, cover and let cool.

6 Lift the nougat from the pan and brush off the excess cornstarch powder. Using a serrated knife, cut the nougat into ¾-inch slices. Cut the slices in pieces and serve, or wrap in wax paper and store in an airtight container for up to 2 weeks.

BELINDA LEONG

PASTRY CHEF / OWNER • B. PATISSERIE • SAN FRANCISCO

she has a sense of gravitas

in her work." That's a compliment not often directed at pastry chefs, but it's how star chef David Kinch praises Belinda Leong, 35. She's become known for reviving and modernizing Old World pastries rarely seen in the United States, like her signature *kouign amann* (kween-yah-MAHN), a sweet layered pastry from France's Brittany region that looks like a gooey, puck-shaped croissant. Leong learned these technically difficult desserts during an apprenticeship with the legendary Pierre Hermé in Paris, then perfected them while she was the pastry chef at Manresa, Kinch's innovative two-Michelin-starred restaurant in Los Gatos, outside San Francisco. "Belinda was way ahead of the trend in this country, reestablishing classic French pastries in a much more contemporary fashion," says Kinch. "She's contemporary but not in a flippant way. There's a great sense of depth in what she does."

The San Francisco native got her start at the Michelin-starred restaurant Gary Danko, where she created desserts for nine years. With no formal pastry training (her background is in graphic arts) and no senior pastry chef to teach her, she consulted books and the Internet to research recipes and took short breaks to apprentice at restaurants like Daniel in New York City. "I remember Belinda always sketching out her desserts during our manager meetings, her mind constantly working," Danko says. Her drawing of an apple-caramel dessert, for instance, is like a scientific diagram revealing a cross section of apple chips, sour-cream ice cream and *joconde* (almond sponge cake) with caramel sauce.

Leong left Gary Danko in 2008 to work her way through Europe at renowned restaurants such as Noma in Copenhagen and haute *pâtisseries* like Bubó in Barcelona. She returned to the Bay Area in 2010 and became the pastry chef at Manresa, but after a year she started to get restless. "I had all this stuff I learned in Europe but couldn't serve at the restaurant," she says. So in 2011, while still at Manresa, she did a *pâtisserie* pop-up. A few months later, she made the radical move of quitting her job to focus on pop-ups. Her roommate at the time, chef Thomas McNaughton, hosted the events at his San Francisco restaurant Flour + Water. "What's amazing is that Belinda can wear two hats: She's a pastry chef who does elegant plated desserts, then switches to elaborate pastries," McNaughton says. These include a bostock (a twice-baked soaked brioche) flavored with passion fruit syrup and a multitextured lemon tart filled with two takes on lemon curd: baked crème brûlée–style and a silky lemon cream (page 90).

Today Leong sells her modern-classic sweets at San Francisco's Ferry Building and at cafés and pop-ups around the Bay Area while preparing to launch her much-anticipated B. Patisserie, scheduled to open by the end of 2012 in the Pacific Heights neighborhood of the city. At B. Patisserie she plans to use her formidable technique and creativity to reinvent homespun desserts like her Chocolate Brownie Cookies (page 98), which have fudgy-crisp edges surrounding an ultra-light cookie center. Leong also has very specific ideas about what her pastry boutique will look like. "I don't want it to be an intimidating jewelry-box shop," she says. "I want everyone to feel comfortable there." Like her pastries, B. Patisserie will be French-influenced but American in spirit. "I want to re-create the life that I had in Paris and bring it back here," Leong says.

CARAMEL
CHIPS

CHOCOLATE
GA

ALMOND
CAKE CROUTONS

> **Belinda was ahead of the trend, reestablishing classic French pastries in a much more modern style. She's contemporary but not in a flippant way. There's a great depth in what she does.**

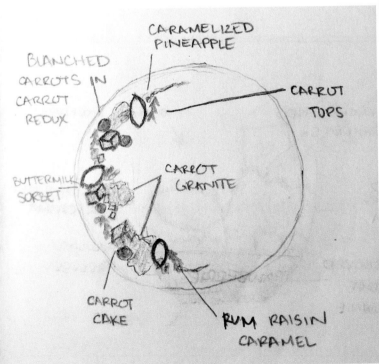

CARAMELIZED PINEAPPLE

BLANCHED CARROTS IN CARROT REDUX

CARROT TOPS

BUTTERMILK SORBET

CARROT GRANITE

CARROT CAKE

RUM RAISIN CARAMEL

"In France, there's almond flour in everything—except clafoutis," Leong says about the rustic dessert of fruit baked in batter. Bucking tradition, she includes the flour in her clafoutis to add texture to the custardy interior.

CHERRY CLAFOUTIS

ACTIVE *25 min* **TOTAL** *1 hr plus cooling* **MAKES** *8 servings*

1 cup granulated sugar, plus more for dusting

5 large eggs

½ vanilla bean, split and seeds scraped

¾ cup all-purpose flour, sifted

¾ cup plus 2 tablespoons almond flour or almond meal

1 teaspoon kosher salt

1 cup whole milk

1 cup heavy cream

12 ounces sweet cherries, pitted

Confectioners' sugar, for dusting

Sweetened whipped cream, for serving

PAIR WITH *Sweet sparkling red wine: 2011 Tenimenti Ca'Bianca Brachetto d'Acqui*

1 Preheat the oven to 350°. Butter a 10-inch round gratin dish and dust it with granulated sugar. In a large bowl, whisk the 1 cup of granulated sugar with the eggs and vanilla seeds. Whisk in the all-purpose flour, almond flour and salt until just incorporated. Add the milk and cream and whisk until light and very smooth, about 3 minutes. Pour the batter into the prepared gratin dish and arrange the cherries on top.

2 Bake for 35 to 40 minutes, until the clafoutis is set and golden. Let cool. Dust with confectioners' sugar, cut into wedges and serve with whipped cream.

MAKE AHEAD *The clafoutis can be wrapped and refrigerated overnight. Bring to room temperature before serving.*

Leong doesn't intentionally make virtuous desserts, but this cake just happens to be gluten-free. It has a remarkable, light texture and an intense almond flavor. Leong suggests using a high-quality almond paste that's at least 66 percent almond. "The cheaper stuff tastes fake," she says.

GLUTEN-FREE ALMOND CAKE

ACTIVE *25 min*   **TOTAL** *1 hr plus cooling*   **MAKES** *6 servings*

9 ounces pure almond paste
2 large eggs
6 tablespoons unsalted butter, melted and cooled slightly
3½ tablespoons cornstarch, sifted
1¼ teaspoons baking powder
2 large egg whites
1½ tablespoons granulated sugar
⅓ cup sliced almonds
Confectioners' sugar, for dusting
Sweetened whipped cream, for serving

PAIR WITH *Citrusy, nutty Italian dessert wine: 2008 Sartarelli Passito*

1 Preheat the oven to 350°. Spray an 8-inch round cake pan with nonstick cooking spray and line the bottom with parchment paper. In the bowl of a standing mixer fitted with the paddle attachment, beat the almond paste with 1 of the eggs until smooth. Add the remaining egg and beat until thick and pale, about 5 minutes. Add the melted butter, cornstarch and baking powder and beat until incorporated. Scrape the almond mixture into a large bowl.

2 In another large bowl, using a handheld electric mixer, beat the egg whites at medium-high speed until opaque and foamy. Gradually beat in the granulated sugar at high speed and continue beating until medium-stiff peaks form, about 3 minutes longer.

3 Using a rubber spatula, gently fold the egg whites into the almond mixture until no streaks remain. Scrape the batter into the prepared pan and sprinkle the sliced almonds on top. Bake the cake for about 35 minutes, until lightly browned and firm. Let cool completely.

4 Unmold the cake and peel off the parchment paper. Transfer the cake to a serving platter, right side up. Dust with confectioners' sugar, cut into wedges and serve with whipped cream.

MAKE AHEAD *The cake can be stored in an airtight container at room temperature for up to 2 days.*

This luscious lemon cream, a staple in Leong's crème brûlée–style lemon tarts, has a bracing tartness. It's lovely as a topping for scones and biscuits at brunch or dolloped on fresh berries for dessert, as in the recipe here.

FRESH BERRIES WITH LEMON CREAM

TOTAL *30 min plus 4 hr chilling*   **MAKES** *8 to 10 servings*

1   teaspoon finely grated lemon zest
¾   cup sugar
¾   cup fresh lemon juice (4 lemons)
4   large eggs plus 1 large egg yolk
Salt
1½   sticks unsalted butter, cubed
Mixed fresh berries, for serving

1 In a medium saucepan, bring 2 inches of water to a boil; keep the water at a simmer over low heat. In a large stainless steel or glass bowl, using your fingers, rub the lemon zest into the sugar. Whisk in the lemon juice, eggs, egg yolk and a pinch of salt. Set the bowl over the simmering water and cook the mixture, stirring, until very thick, 5 to 7 minutes. Scrape the cream into a medium bowl.

2 Add 3 tablespoons of the butter to the cream. Using an immersion blender, puree until the cream is smooth. Add the remaining butter and puree until incorporated. Press a sheet of plastic wrap directly onto the surface of the cream and refrigerate until well chilled, about 4 hours. Spoon over fresh berries and serve.

MAKE AHEAD *The lemon cream can be refrigerated for up to 2 days.*

Crémeux (French for "creamy") is a dense, soft, classic pudding that's the new darling of many American pastry chefs. Leong gives her super-chocolaty version a salty edge; it's delightful with fruit, cookies and ice cream, or topped with a dab of whipped cream.

BITTERSWEET CHOCOLATE CRÉMEUX

TOTAL *30 min plus 6 hr chilling*   **MAKES** *8 servings*

1½ cups heavy cream
1½ cups whole milk
 5 large egg yolks
½ cup sugar
 2 teaspoons kosher salt
 9 ounces dark chocolate (70 to 72 percent cacao), such as Valrhona Guanaja, finely chopped
Sweetened whipped cream and chocolate shavings, for serving

PAIR WITH *Toffee- and chocolate-scented fortified wine: Broadbent 5-Year Reserve Madeira*

1 In a medium saucepan, bring the cream and milk to a simmer. Remove from the heat. In a medium bowl, whisk the egg yolks with the sugar and salt. Gradually whisk in the hot cream. Transfer the mixture to the saucepan and cook over moderately low heat, stirring constantly with a wooden spoon, until the custard is slightly thickened and coats the back of the spoon, about 5 minutes.

2 Strain the custard through a fine sieve into a heatproof bowl. Add the chopped chocolate and let stand until melted, about 2 minutes. Whisk vigorously until smooth, then pour the *crémeux* into a shallow glass or ceramic dish. Press a sheet of plastic wrap directly onto the surface of the *crémeux* and refrigerate until set, at least 6 hours or overnight. Spoon the *crémeux* into glasses, top with sweetened whipped cream and chocolate shavings and serve.

MAKE AHEAD *The* crémeux *can be refrigerated for up to 2 days.*

Leong started to incorporate wild greens and herbs into her desserts in 2009 during a foraging-focused internship at the world-renowned Noma restaurant in Copenhagen. When sorrel's in season, she uses the tart, lemony green to flavor her tangy sherbet, but mint, thyme and basil are also terrific.

LEMON & FRESH SORREL SHERBET

TOTAL *30 min plus 5 hr chilling and freezing*   **MAKES** *about 1 quart*

1¼ teaspoons unflavored powdered gelatin
1 cup fresh lemon juice (5 to 6 lemons)
1½ cups sugar
2¼ cups whole milk
5 large sorrel leaves
2 teaspoons finely grated lemon zest

1 In a small bowl, sprinkle the gelatin over the lemon juice and let stand until softened, about 5 minutes.

2 In a medium saucepan, combine the sugar with 1½ cups of water and bring to a boil. Simmer over moderate heat until the sugar is dissolved, 2 to 3 minutes. Remove from the heat and whisk in the lemon juice mixture. Let cool completely, then refrigerate until well chilled, about 2 hours.

3 In a blender, combine the lemon mixture with the milk and sorrel and puree until almost smooth, about 30 seconds. Strain the mixture through a fine sieve into a bowl and stir in the lemon zest.

4 Pour the sherbet mixture into an ice cream maker and freeze according to the manufacturer's instructions. Transfer to an airtight container, cover and freeze the sherbet until it is firm, at least 2 hours, before serving.

VARIATION *For Lemon & Fresh Mint Sherbet, replace the sorrel leaves with ½ cup of lightly packed mint leaves.*

MAKE AHEAD *The sherbet can be kept in the freezer for up to 2 weeks.*

Brown butter, made by warming butter in a skillet until deeply golden, adds a wonderful nutty flavor to this chunky, streusel-like topping. Sprinkle the crumble on vanilla ice cream for outrageously good sundaes.

VANILLA ICE CREAM WITH BROWN BUTTER CRUMBLE

ACTIVE *20 min*   **TOTAL** *1 hr 40 min plus cooling*   **MAKES** *about 3 cups*

1 stick plus 6 tablespoons
   unsalted butter
½ cup granulated sugar
1½ cups all-purpose flour
¾ cup dark brown sugar
½ cup almond meal or almond flour
1¼ teaspoons fine sea salt
Vanilla ice cream and chocolate sauce,
   for serving

1 In a small saucepan, cook the butter over moderate heat, shaking the pan occasionally, until the butter is nutty-smelling and golden and the foam subsides, about 5 minutes. Pour the brown butter into a heatproof bowl and stir in the granulated sugar. Let cool slightly.

2 Line a baking sheet with parchment paper. In a medium bowl, whisk the flour with the brown sugar, almond meal and salt. Stir in the brown butter mixture until evenly moistened crumbs form. Transfer to the prepared baking sheet and, using your hands, press the crumbs into an even layer a scant ⅓ inch thick. Cover with plastic wrap and refrigerate until well chilled, about 1 hour.

3 Preheat the oven to 350°. Break the dough into small chunks and bake for about 20 minutes, until it is golden and slightly dry. Let cool completely, then serve the crumble over vanilla ice cream and chocolate sauce.

MAKE AHEAD *The crumble can be refrigerated in an airtight container for up to 1 week.*

Food&Wine *editor in chief Dana Cowin, a cookie connoisseur, declares these double-chocolate ones the most delicious she's ever had. They're like crispy-chewy brownies in cookie form.*

CHOCOLATE BROWNIE COOKIES

ACTIVE *30 min*   **TOTAL** *2 hr 30 min plus cooling*   **MAKES** *about 3 dozen cookies*

  1 *pound semisweet chocolate, chopped*
  4 *tablespoons unsalted butter*
  4 *large eggs, at room temperature*
1½ *cups sugar*
  1 *teaspoon pure vanilla extract*
  ¼ *teaspoon salt*
  ½ *cup all-purpose flour, sifted*
  ½ *teaspoon baking powder*
One 12-ounce bag semisweet chocolate chips

1 In a large bowl set over a saucepan of simmering water, melt the chopped chocolate with the butter, stirring a few times, until smooth, about 7 minutes.

2 In another large bowl, using a hand-held electric mixer, beat the eggs with the sugar at medium speed until thick and pale, about 5 minutes. Beat in the vanilla and salt. Using a rubber spatula, fold in the melted chocolate, then fold in the flour and baking powder. Stir in the chocolate chips. Scrape the batter into a shallow baking dish, cover and freeze until well chilled and firm, about 1 hour.

3 Preheat the oven to 350° and line 2 baking sheets with parchment paper. Working in batches, scoop 2-tablespoon-size mounds of dough onto the prepared baking sheets about 2 inches apart. Bake for about 10 minutes, until the cookies are dry around the edges and cracked on top. Let the cookies cool on the baking sheets for 10 minutes, then transfer to a rack to cool completely before serving.

MAKE AHEAD *The cookies can be stored in an airtight container at room temperature for up to 4 days.*

Leong made many kinds of ganache (a rich, smooth chocolate-and-cream mixture) during her time at the venerable Pierre Hermé pâtisserie in Paris. Here, she slow-roasts white chocolate, which adds an enticing caramel flavor to the supercreamy ganache filling in her truffles.

ROASTED WHITE CHOCOLATE & COFFEE TRUFFLES

TOTAL *4 hr plus 4 hr 15 min chilling*　　**MAKES** *about 2 dozen truffles*

9　ounces Valrhona Ivoire white baking chocolate, chopped
½　cup heavy cream
1　tablespoon freshly ground coffee
Salt
Unsweetened cocoa powder, for dusting
7　ounces bittersweet chocolate, chopped

1 Preheat the oven to 225°. In a medium stainless steel bowl, roast the chopped white chocolate for 3 hours, stirring every 15 minutes, until golden.

2 In a medium saucepan, bring the cream to a simmer over moderate heat. Remove from the heat, add the ground coffee and a pinch of salt and let steep for 2 minutes. Strain the cream through a fine sieve into the bowl with the roasted white chocolate and whisk until blended. Scrape the ganache into a shallow baking dish and press a piece of plastic wrap directly onto the surface. Refrigerate until firm, at least 3 hours.

3 Line a large rimmed baking sheet with parchment paper. Using a 1-inch ice cream scoop, drop heaping teaspoons of the ganache onto the prepared baking sheet. Moisten your hands with ice water and roll the ganache into balls. Refrigerate until very firm, about 1 hour.

4 Spoon the cocoa powder into a small bowl. In a medium bowl set over a saucepan of simmering water, melt the bittersweet chocolate over moderately low heat, about 3 to 5 minutes. Remove from the heat and stir the chocolate slowly until glossy and just starting to thicken, about 5 minutes.

5 Using a fork, dip each truffle in the melted chocolate, coat it in the cocoa powder, then return it to the baking sheet. Refrigerate the truffles to set the shells, about 15 minutes, before serving.

MAKE AHEAD *The coated truffles can be refrigerated for up to 3 days.*

Instead of adding dried fruit to her crunchy granola, Leong creates chewy-sticky clusters of oats, nuts and poppy seeds. She serves the granola with her Greek yogurt panna cotta, but it's also fabulous with plain yogurt or as a snack by itself.

ALMOND–POPPY SEED GRANOLA

ACTIVE *10 min*   **TOTAL** *40 min plus cooling*   **MAKES** *about 4 cups*

2 cups rolled oats
1 cup sliced almonds
½ cup plus 2 tablespoons
   all-purpose flour
½ cup light brown sugar
2 tablespoons poppy seeds
1 teaspoon kosher salt
1 stick unsalted butter
¼ cup pure maple syrup
2 tablespoons honey, warmed

1 Preheat the oven to 300° and line a rimmed baking sheet with parchment paper. In a large bowl, toss the oats with the almonds, flour, brown sugar, poppy seeds and salt. In a small saucepan, melt the butter in the maple syrup, then add to the oat mixture and stir until thoroughly coated. Spread the granola on the prepared baking sheet.

2 Bake the granola in the center of the oven for 10 minutes. Stir the granola, then drizzle the honey over the top. Bake for 20 minutes longer, stirring once more, until golden and nearly dry. Turn off the oven and prop the door open halfway; let the granola cool completely in the oven, stirring occasionally, before serving.

MAKE AHEAD *The granola can be stored in an airtight container at room temperature for up to 3 weeks.*

When San Francisco's revered Four Barrel coffeehouse asked Leong to make bran muffins for them, she added bran to her favorite carrot cake recipe. The result is an extraordinarily fluffy bran muffin that stays moist for days.

CARROT-BRAN MUFFINS

ACTIVE *20 min*   **TOTAL** *50 min plus cooling*   **MAKES** *18 muffins*

2 cups all-purpose flour, sifted
2 teaspoons baking powder
¾ teaspoon baking soda
1 teaspoon kosher salt
2 cups sugar
1 cup vegetable oil
4 large eggs
1 cup wheat bran
1 pound carrots, shredded
     (2½ cups)

1 Preheat the oven to 350° and line 18 muffin cups with paper or foil liners. In a medium bowl, whisk the flour with the baking powder, baking soda and salt. In a large bowl, whisk the sugar with the oil and eggs. Whisk in the dry ingredients until just incorporated, then stir in the wheat bran and carrots.

2 Spoon the batter into the prepared muffin cups and bake for 18 to 20 minutes, until a toothpick inserted in the center of a muffin comes out with a few moist crumbs attached. Let the muffins cool for 10 minutes in the pan, then turn them out onto a rack to cool completely before serving.

MAKE AHEAD *The muffins can be wrapped in plastic and stored at room temperature overnight.*

NICO MONDAY + AMELIA O'REILLY

CHEFS / OWNERS • THE MARKET RESTAURANT • GLOUCESTER, MASSACHUSETTS

they have such a wonderful sensibility," says legendary chef Alice Waters. She is referring to her godson Nico Monday and his fiancée, Amelia O'Reilly, the talented chefs and owners of the Market Restaurant on Lobster Cove in Gloucester, Massachusetts. Monday, 30, and O'Reilly, 29, are their generation's answer to Alice Waters: Both cooked at Chez Panisse, Waters's pioneering restaurant in Berkeley, California, and have been deeply influenced by their mentor's local, sustainable ethos. But instead of importing California style to New England, they serve simple, outstanding, unpretentious food that shows real respect for the Market's setting, a weathered wood building perched over the Annisquam River in America's oldest fishing port.

"What Nico and Amelia are doing is very true to the place—especially a place with as much history and natural beauty as Gloucester," says Tony Maws. The chef at Craigie on Main in Cambridge, Massachusetts, Maws frequently makes the hour-long drive to eat at the Market Restaurant during its short (May to October) season. *Top Chef* judge and *Food & Wine* special projects producer Gail Simmons, who vacations in Gloucester with her husband and his family, fell in love with the restaurant on her first visit a couple of years ago and has been a regular ever since. "The Market is totally unlike anything in the area," Simmons says. "It's in a beautiful location with food to match. It's just what summer in New England should be."

Before cooking at Chez Panisse, Monday spent two years working in France and Italy, including an apprenticeship at star butcher Dario Cecchini's shop outside Florence. He met O'Reilly when she came to work in the Chez Panisse kitchen after graduating from San Francisco's California Culinary Academy in 2006. (Monday's parents also met at Chez Panisse, waiting tables in the 1970s.)

The couple opened the Market Restaurant in 2010 when O'Reilly learned that the space, a general store turned greasy spoon just down the street from where she grew up, was vacant. They kept the building's rustic feel, so that it still looks like one of many old seafood shacks in the area, but began sourcing incredibly fresh, ultralocal ingredients—lobster pulled up in traps from the Market's balcony; scallops caught just hundreds of yards out in the water, delivered still twitching. "Gloucester has a rich fishing tradition," Monday says, "and it's exciting to have such amazing seafood right at our doorstep."

The chefs do everything by hand, including pickling vegetables, butchering meat and smoking their own fish to add to a creamy fresh-corn chowder with potatoes from a nearby farm (page 110). Monday and O'Reilly change the menu every single day, paring it down to just three or four starters and three main courses. For instance, they might simmer beautiful count neck clams in white wine perfumed with saffron, then serve them with a basil-inflected tomato confit and baguette toasts (page 120). There's always a local selection of cheeses and one or two fruit desserts, such as a tender, light buttermilk cake filled with tart, just-picked blackberries (page 128).

The result: a less-is-more feeling of abundance. "There are no bells and whistles or hootenanny at the Market Restaurant—none of which necessarily makes anything tastier," says Tony Maws. "The food that they do just makes sense to me. It's beautiful, uncomplicated and flat-out delicious."

THE MARKET RESTAURANT
ON LOBSTER COVE
SEPTEMBER 2011

½ DOZEN CARAQUET OYSTERS
WITH MIGNONETTE
$13

BRAISED OXTAIL ARANCINE, ROASTED PEPPER
RELISH AND ROCKET SALAD
$10

APPLE ST. FARM ESCAROLE WITH POUNDED
GARLIC AND ANCHOVY VINAIGRETTE AND CROUTON
$9

HOUSE SMOKED HADDOCK CHOWDER WITH
CORN, LEEKS AND CHERVIL BUTTER
$10

PORK CHOP WITH BUTTERNUT SQUASH
PUREE AND GREENS
$27

PAN-FRIED GREY SOLE WITH NEW POTATOES,
MARINATED BEETS, BASIL AND AIOLI
$27

POTATO AND GRUYERE GRIDDLECAKES WITH CHARD,
CHIVE CRÉME FRAICHE AND A POACHED FARM EGG
$20

CAITLIN'S
RUSSELL ORCHARD
FIRST LIGHT FARM
APPLETON FARM
VALLEY VIEW FARM
THE FOOD PROJECT
A & J KING BAKERY

> **What Nico and Amelia are doing is very true to the place—especially a place with as much history and natural beauty as Gloucester. The food is uncomplicated and just flat-out delicious.**

Any local smoked fish, from haddock to trout, works well in this creamy chowder studded with corn kernels and tender chunks of potato. The recipe is also terrific made with fresh cod or sole and a little bacon for smokiness.

SMOKED FISH CHOWDER

ACTIVE *30 min*   **TOTAL** *50 min*   **MAKES** *6 to 8 servings*

2 ears of corn, kernels cut from the cobs

1½ pounds large red-skinned potatoes, peeled and cut into ½-inch dice

3 tablespoons unsalted butter

2 fennel bulbs, cored and thinly sliced, fronds reserved and chopped

2 large leeks, white and pale green parts only, cut into ¼-inch dice

1 large onion, thinly sliced

2 thyme sprigs

1 bay leaf

Salt and freshly ground pepper

1 quart plus 3 cups milk

1 cup heavy cream

1 pound smoked fish, such as haddock, mackerel, bluefish or trout, skinned and flaked

PAIR WITH *Minerally northern Italian white: 2011 Kellerei Cantina Terlan Pinot Bianco*

1 In a large saucepan of salted boiling water, cook the corn until just tender, about 1 minute. With a slotted spoon, transfer the corn to a bowl. Add the potatoes to the boiling water and cook until tender, about 6 minutes. Drain the potatoes and add to the bowl.

2 In a large pot, melt the butter. Add the fennel slices, leeks, onion, thyme and bay leaf and season with salt and pepper. Cover and cook over low heat, stirring occasionally, until the vegetables are softened, about 10 minutes. Add the milk, cream, corn and potatoes and simmer for about 3 minutes, smashing some of the potatoes to thicken the soup. Discard the thyme sprigs and bay leaf. Add the fish and simmer until heated through, about 2 minutes. Season lightly with salt and pepper. Ladle the chowder into bowls, garnish with fennel fronds and serve.

MAKE AHEAD *The chowder (without the smoked fish) can be refrigerated for up to 2 days. Reheat gently, add the fish and serve.*

This perfect summer salad combines both fresh and dried figs in a sweet-tangy vinaigrette. O'Reilly recommends using purple Mission figs for their balance of acidity and sweetness. "The brown figs are fat and one-note sweet," she says.

BUTTER LETTUCE & ROMANO BEAN SALAD WITH FIG VINAIGRETTE

ACTIVE *20 min*   **TOTAL** *50 min*   **MAKES** *4 to 6 servings*

2 dried figs, finely chopped
½ cup hazelnuts
2 tablespoons red wine vinegar
1 tablespoon minced shallot
1 teaspoon Dijon mustard
Kosher salt and freshly ground pepper
¼ cup finely chopped parsley
3 tablespoons extra-virgin olive oil
½ pound romano beans
1 head of butter lettuce, torn into
    bite-size pieces
8 fresh figs, quartered lengthwise

1 Preheat the oven to 325°. In a small bowl, cover the dried figs with warm water and let them stand until they are plumped, about 20 minutes.

2 Meanwhile, spread the hazelnuts in a pie plate and toast in the oven for about 15 minutes, until the nuts are fragrant and the skins blister. Transfer to a clean kitchen towel and let cool slightly, then rub them together to remove the skins. Let cool completely, then coarsely chop.

3 In a large bowl, whisk the vinegar with the shallot and mustard and season with salt and pepper. Let stand for 10 minutes. Drain the plumped figs and whisk them into the vinaigrette along with the parsley and olive oil.

4 In a medium saucepan of salted boiling water, cook the romano beans until crisp-tender, about 4 minutes. Drain and cool under running water, then pat the beans dry. Cut the beans into ½-inch pieces on the diagonal.

5 Add the butter lettuce, hazelnuts and romano beans to the vinaigrette and toss well; season with salt and pepper. Transfer the salad to bowls, top with the fresh figs and serve right away.

The warm, garlicky anchovy dressing here is fantastic with an assortment of juicy, peak-season tomatoes. To finish the dish, O'Reilly and Monday top it with tangy pickled shallots and an oozy, soft-boiled egg.

HEIRLOOM TOMATO SALAD WITH ANCHOVY VINAIGRETTE

TOTAL *30 min*   **MAKES** *4 servings*

¼ cup extra-virgin olive oil
4 anchovies, minced
1 garlic clove, minced
1 teaspoon finely grated lemon zest
1 medium shallot, thinly sliced
2 tablespoons red wine vinegar
2 large eggs
1½ pounds assorted heirloom tomatoes—large ones sliced, small ones halved
Fleur de sel and freshly ground pepper
Flat-leaf parsley and marjoram leaves, for serving

PAIR WITH *Vibrant California Sauvignon Blanc: 2011 Joel Gott*

1 In a small skillet, combine the olive oil, anchovies, garlic and lemon zest.

2 In a small bowl, toss the shallot with the vinegar and let stand for 10 minutes.

3 Bring a small saucepan of water to a boil. Turn the heat to low, and when the water is simmering, gently place the eggs in the water. Cook for 6 minutes, until lightly boiled. Have an ice bath ready near the stove. Using a slotted spoon, plunge the eggs in the ice bath and let cool for 2 minutes. Peel the eggs.

4 Arrange the tomatoes on 4 plates and season them with fleur de sel and pepper. Sprinkle the shallot slices and vinegar over the tomatoes.

5 Warm the anchovy dressing over moderate heat to a gentle simmer; pour over the tomatoes. Halve the eggs crosswise and place a half on each plate. Scatter the parsley and marjoram over the salads and serve at once.

"All the things that are wonderful about spring are in this one dish," says O'Reilly. She suggests substituting English peas, even frozen ones, for the fava beans if favas aren't available or you don't want to bother shelling them. "My mom buys favas and they just sit in the bag," she says.

WARM ASPARAGUS SALAD WITH FAVA BEANS & FRESH RICOTTA

TOTAL *40 min* **MAKES** *4 servings*

1   cup fresh ricotta cheese
1   teaspoon finely grated lemon zest
Kosher salt and freshly ground black
      pepper
1¼ pounds fresh fava beans, shelled
      (about 1 cup)
1   tablespoon finely chopped parsley
1   tablespoon finely chopped mint
2   tablespoons extra-virgin olive oil
1   pound thin asparagus
1   tablespoon fresh lemon juice
Fleur de sel, for sprinkling

PAIR WITH *Zippy, zesty Grüner Veltliner: 2011 Sepp Moser Sepp*

1 In a medium bowl, whisk the ricotta cheese with the lemon zest and season with kosher salt and black pepper.

2 In a medium saucepan of salted boiling water, cook the fava beans until the skins start to loosen, about 2 minutes. Drain and cool under running water, then squeeze the fava beans from their skins. In a medium bowl, toss the favas with the parsley, mint and 1 tablespoon of the olive oil; season with kosher salt and black pepper.

3 In a large saucepan of salted boiling water, blanch the asparagus until crisp-tender, 2 to 3 minutes, then drain. In a medium bowl, toss the asparagus with the lemon juice and the remaining 1 tablespoon of olive oil; season with kosher salt and black pepper. Transfer the asparagus to plates and spoon the ricotta and favas over the top. Sprinkle the salads with fleur de sel and serve.

Monday and O'Reilly say they summoned their "inner Moroccan" to spice this vegetarian dish with cumin, coriander and mustard seeds. They serve the baked eggplant at the Market both as a first course and as a main along with couscous, chickpeas and charmoula (a punchy, cilantro-based Moroccan sauce).

SPICE-BRAISED GINGERED EGGPLANT WITH MINT YOGURT

ACTIVE *1 hr 15 min*   **TOTAL** *2 hr plus cooling*   **MAKES** *4 main-course or 6 first-course servings*

1 cup plain whole-milk yogurt
¼ cup finely chopped mint
1 teaspoon red wine vinegar
Kosher salt
Vegetable oil, for frying
Six 6-ounce Italian or Japanese
  eggplants, halved lengthwise
1 tablespoon cumin seeds
1 tablespoon coriander seeds
1 teaspoon yellow mustard seeds
Two 14-ounce cans diced tomatoes
2 ounces fresh ginger—peeled,
  chopped and smashed
6 garlic cloves, finely chopped
1 jalapeño, seeded and finely
  chopped
½ cup chopped cilantro, plus
  more for garnish
½ cup chopped parsley, plus
  more for garnish

PAIR WITH *Juicy, red berry–inflected Pinot Noir: 2009 Cloudline Cellars*

1 In a medium bowl, whisk the yogurt with the mint and vinegar and season with salt. Cover and refrigerate.

2 Preheat the oven to 400°. In a large, deep skillet, heat ½ inch of oil until shimmering. Add half of the eggplant, cut side down, and fry over moderate heat, turning once, until lightly golden, about 10 minutes. Transfer the eggplant to paper towels to drain and season with salt. Repeat with the remaining eggplant.

3 In a small skillet, toast the cumin and coriander seeds over moderate heat, stirring, until fragrant, about 2 minutes. Transfer to a spice grinder and let cool completely, then finely grind the spices. Add the mustard seeds to the skillet and toast over moderate heat until they start to pop, about 2 minutes.

4 In a 9-by-13-inch ceramic baking dish, mix the tomatoes with the ground spices, toasted mustard seeds, ginger, garlic, jalapeño, 2 teaspoons of salt, 1 cup of water and the ½ cup each of chopped cilantro and parsley. Arrange the eggplant halves cut side down in the sauce

and cover tightly with foil. Bake for 30 minutes, turning the eggplant once, until tender. Remove the foil and bake for 15 minutes longer. Let the eggplant cool completely in the sauce.

5 Transfer the eggplant to plates. Spoon the tomato sauce on top and garnish with chopped cilantro and parsley. Drizzle the yogurt sauce over the eggplant and serve.

MAKE AHEAD *The eggplant can be refrigerated in the sauce overnight. Bring to room temperature before serving.*

The clams' natural juices, flavored with saffron, make a wonderful broth; a drizzle of basil-scented tomato oil enhances the flavor even more. At the Market, O'Reilly and Monday use count neck clams, which have beautiful black-and-white shells, but any small to medium-size clams will do.

CLAMS WITH HOT PEPPER, SAFFRON & TOMATO CONFIT

TOTAL *50 min* **MAKES** *4 servings*

2 pints cherry tomatoes
1 cup extra-virgin olive oil
½ cup lightly packed basil leaves
8 garlic cloves—4 crushed, 4 minced
Kosher salt
½ large baguette, sliced ¾ inch thick on the diagonal
3 dozen littleneck clams, scrubbed
1 cup dry white wine
2 tablespoons unsalted butter
1 teaspoon crushed red pepper
Pinch of saffron threads
½ cup finely chopped parsley
1 tablespoon finely chopped marjoram or oregano
1 small plum tomato, halved
Fleur de sel, for sprinkling

PAIR WITH *Robust, juicy rosé: 2011 Bisson Ciliegiolo Rosato*

1 In a medium saucepan, combine the cherry tomatoes with the olive oil, basil leaves, crushed garlic and 1 tablespoon of kosher salt. Cook over low heat until the tomatoes just start to soften but the skins are still intact, about 20 minutes. Let the tomatoes cool slightly.

2 Preheat the oven to 350°. Brush the baguette slices with some of the tomato oil and arrange them on a baking sheet. Bake for about 8 minutes, until they are lightly browned and just crisp.

3 In a large saucepan, heat 2 tablespoons of the tomato oil until shimmering. Add the minced garlic, clams and wine and bring to a boil. Cover and simmer over high heat until the clams open, about 5 minutes. Discard any clams that do not open. Add the butter, crushed red pepper and saffron and cook, stirring, until the butter is melted, about 30 seconds. Stir in the parsley and marjoram.

4 Ladle the clams and broth into bowls and spoon the tomato confit and some of the oil on top (reserve the remaining oil for later use). Rub the baguette toasts with the halved plum tomato and sprinkle with fleur de sel. Serve right away.

These crispy cakes have big hunks of succulent seafood. Monday and O'Reilly love haddock, a sustainable fish with sweet, firm white flesh. The accompanying basil mayonnaise is a big improvement on basic tartar sauce.

HADDOCK & SHRIMP CAKES WITH BASIL MAYONNAISE

TOTAL *50 min*   **MAKES** *4 servings*

½ cup basil leaves
½ cup mayonnaise
Kosher salt and freshly ground
     black pepper
¾ pound skinless haddock or
     cod fillet, cut into ¼-inch pieces
½ pound medium shrimp—
     shelled, deveined and cut into
     ¼-inch pieces
½ cup panko (Japanese bread
     crumbs)
¼ cup heavy cream
1 large egg, lightly beaten
2 tablespoons finely chopped
     parsley
2 tablespoons finely chopped chives
1 teaspoon finely grated lemon zest
Pinch of cayenne pepper
4 tablespoons unsalted butter
2 tablespoons vegetable oil

PAIR WITH *Dry, floral Provençal rosé: 2011 Domaine du Bagnol*

1 In a small saucepan of boiling water, blanch the basil for 30 seconds. Drain and rinse it under cold running water. Squeeze the excess water from the basil and transfer the basil to a blender. Add the mayonnaise and puree. Transfer to a bowl and season with salt and black pepper. Refrigerate the basil mayonnaise until lightly chilled.

2 In a large bowl, combine the haddock and shrimp with the panko, heavy cream, egg, chopped parsley and chives, lemon zest, cayenne, 1½ teaspoons of salt and ½ teaspoon of black pepper. Form the mixture into eight ½-cup cakes, about 3 inches in diameter.

3 In a large cast-iron skillet, melt 2 tablespoons of the butter in the oil. Add 4 of the fish cakes and fry over moderately high heat until browned and crisp, about 3 minutes per side. Using a slotted spoon, transfer the fish cakes to paper towels to drain. Repeat with the remaining butter and fish cakes, then transfer the cakes to a platter and serve at once, with the basil mayonnaise.

MAKE AHEAD *The basil mayonnaise can be refrigerated overnight.*

A riff on the classic Venetian dish sarde in saor, *this recipe combines meaty swordfish with vinegared onions and smoky grilled fennel. Look for swordfish steaks that have a nice sheen and are relatively thin; they're more tender than heftier steaks, which can be mealy.*

GRILLED SWORDFISH WITH TANGY ONIONS & FENNEL

ACTIVE *35 min*   **TOTAL** *1 hr*   **MAKES** *4 servings*

¼ cup currants
¼ cup pine nuts
¼ cup extra-virgin olive oil, plus
      more for brushing
4 red onions (1½ pounds),
      thinly sliced
Kosher salt and freshly ground pepper
1 cup dry white wine
½ cup white wine vinegar
1½ tablespoons sugar
1 bay leaf
2 small fennel bulbs, cut through the
      cores into ¾-inch-thick wedges
Four 6-ounce swordfish steaks, about
      1 inch thick

PAIR WITH *Tangy, peach-scented white: 2010 Cold Heaven Santa Ynez Valley Viognier*

1 In a small bowl, soak the currants in warm water until plumped, about 15 minutes, then drain them. In a small skillet, toast the pine nuts over moderate heat until lightly golden, about 4 minutes.

2 In a large, deep skillet, heat the ¼ cup of olive oil until shimmering. Add the onions and a generous pinch each of salt and pepper and cook over moderate heat, stirring occasionally, until the onions are softened and light golden, about 15 minutes. Add the wine, vinegar, sugar and bay leaf and simmer for 10 minutes, stirring occasionally. Discard the bay leaf and keep the onions warm.

3 Meanwhile, light a grill or preheat a grill pan. Brush the fennel wedges with olive oil and season with salt and pepper. Grill the fennel over moderate heat, turning occasionally, until crisp-tender and lightly charred, about 10 minutes. Transfer to a plate.

4 Brush the swordfish steaks with olive oil and season with salt and pepper. Grill the fish over moderately high heat until nicely browned outside and just white throughout, about 3 minutes per side. Spoon the onions onto plates and arrange the swordfish steaks on top. Scatter the currants and pine nuts over the fish and serve with the grilled fennel.

The combination of juicy, pan-seared pork chops and sweet-savory peach relish is incredibly good. Be sure to use firm, ripe peaches for the relish or else they'll get mushy during pickling.

SAGE-RUBBED PORK CHOPS WITH PICKLED PEACH RELISH

ACTIVE *35 min*   **TOTAL** *2 hr*   **MAKES** *4 servings*

2 cups white wine vinegar
¼ cup sugar
2 tablespoons yellow mustard seeds
1 bay leaf
1 tablespoon whole black
    peppercorns, plus 1 tablespoon
    coarsely ground black pepper
Kosher salt
4 large ripe but firm peaches,
    pitted and cut into ½-inch dice
3 tablespoons extra-virgin olive oil
20 small sage leaves,
    plus 1 tablespoon chopped sage
Four 1-inch-thick, bone-in pork rib
    chops (10 to 12 ounces each)

PAIR WITH *Full-bodied Rhône white: 2011 Kermit Lynch Sunflower Cuvée Côtes du Rhône Blanc*

1 In a large saucepan, combine the vinegar with 1½ cups of water and the sugar, mustard seeds, bay leaf, 1 tablespoon of whole peppercorns and 2 tablespoons of salt; bring to a boil to dissolve the sugar. Put the diced peaches in a large heatproof bowl and pour the hot brine over them. Let the peaches stand for 1 hour, then refrigerate them for about 30 minutes, until chilled.

2 Meanwhile, in a small bowl, combine 1 tablespoon of the oil with the chopped sage, coarsely ground pepper and 1 tablespoon plus 1 teaspoon of salt. Rub the mixture all over the chops and let stand for 30 minutes.

3 Preheat the oven to 400°. In a large ovenproof skillet, heat 1 tablespoon of the olive oil until shimmering. Add the pork chops and cook over moderately high heat until browned, 3 minutes per side. Transfer the skillet to the oven and roast for 5 minutes, until an instant-read thermometer inserted in the thickest part of the meat nearest the bone registers 145°. Transfer the chops to a plate to rest for 10 minutes.

4 Meanwhile, in a medium skillet, heat the remaining 1 tablespoon of oil. Add the sage leaves and cook over moderate heat until crisp, about 1 minute per side.

5 Put a pork chop on each plate. Using a slotted spoon, top each chop with about ½ cup of the pickled peaches. Garnish with the fried sage leaves and serve.

MAKE AHEAD *The pickled peaches can be refrigerated for up to 1 week.*

Light and moist, with an irresistible crispy top, this buttermilk cake has sweet-tart berries in every bite and takes just 20 minutes of prep. It will become your go-to cake whenever blackberries (or even raspberries) are in season.

BUTTERMILK CAKE WITH BLACKBERRIES

ACTIVE *20 min*   **TOTAL** *1 hr plus cooling*   **MAKES** *one 9-inch cake*

- 4 tablespoons unsalted butter, softened, plus more for greasing
- 1 cup all-purpose flour
- ½ teaspoon baking powder
- ½ teaspoon baking soda
- ¼ teaspoon salt
- ⅔ cup plus 1½ tablespoons sugar
- 1 large egg, at room temperature
- 1 teaspoon pure vanilla extract
- ½ cup buttermilk, at room temperature
- 1¼ cups blackberries, plus more for serving
- Sweetened whipped cream, for serving

1 Preheat the oven to 400°. Butter a 9-inch round cake pan and line the bottom with parchment paper. Butter the parchment.

2 In a small bowl, whisk the flour, baking powder, baking soda and salt. In a large bowl, using a handheld electric mixer, beat the 4 tablespoons of butter with ⅔ cup of the sugar at medium-high speed until fluffy, 3 minutes. Beat in the egg and vanilla. At low speed, beat in the buttermilk and dry ingredients in 3 alternating batches, ending with the dry ingredients; do not overbeat. Gently fold the batter just until blended, then scrape into the prepared pan; smooth the top.

3 Scatter the 1¼ cups of blackberries over the batter; lightly press them in. Sprinkle the remaining 1½ tablespoons of sugar over the cake. Bake for about 30 minutes, until a cake tester inserted in the center comes out clean.

4 Transfer the cake to a rack to cool for 10 minutes, then turn out the cake and remove the paper. Turn the cake right side up and let cool completely. Serve the buttermilk cake with whipped cream and more blackberries.

BRYANT NG

CHEF / OWNER • THE SPICE TABLE • LOS ANGELES

named a food & wine Best New Chef in 2012, Bryant Ng has had a spectacular rise in the food world. *Los Angeles Times* restaurant critic Jonathan Gold calls him "a startlingly good new chef, reworking the funky, perfumed flavors of his Singaporean heritage with the kind of technique you might expect from a veteran of places like Mozza and Daniel—with fetishes for sustainable produce and modern wood-powered cooking."

Born in Los Angeles in 1977 to immigrant parents (mother from Hong Kong, father from Singapore), Ng got his start in the business by helping his parents run a typical Chinese-American restaurant in the San Fernando Valley that served egg rolls and General Tso's chicken—washing dishes and peeling shrimp. "I not only observed how to work a wok station, I saw how difficult it was to have a restaurant," Ng says. "I wasn't delusional about what it would take to open my own place." He majored in molecular biology at UCLA, but left behind a career in biotech consulting to study at Le Cordon Bleu in Paris when he was 25.

All his culinary training since then has been in Eurocentric kitchens: La Folie in San Francisco, Restaurant Daniel in New York, Campanile and Pizzeria Mozza in Los Angeles. Yet for his own restaurant, Ng returned to his roots, drawing inspiration from the boldly flavored food his father introduced him to on their trips to Singapore—specifically, the street stands that entranced him as a boy. "I remember going to a hawker center called the Satay Club, Singapore's take on an outdoor food court," Ng says. "There were all these street vendors cooking different things: an Indian guy making roti, a Malaysian guy grilling satays. That stuck in my head."

At the Spice Table, which opened in the Little Tokyo neighborhood of Los Angeles in 2011, he paid tribute to that seminal childhood memory by installing a custom-made satay grill at the front of the restaurant. Fueled with almond wood and charcoal, the grill wafts fragrant smoke throughout the brick-exposed interior. "I try to grill everything," he says. "I end every sentence with 'throw it on the grill.'"

With that massive grill Ng turns out dishes that have the soul of Asian street food—like his Southeast Asian rib eye steaks marinated in anchovies, dry mustard, ginger and brown sugar (page 146)—while seamlessly incorporating what he learned from his experience in high-end kitchens. He makes his own headcheese, something he picked up from Daniel Boulud at Restaurant Daniel, but mixes in Asian herbs like cilantro and serves it with pickled mustard greens.

Ng's cooking also pays homage to his wife's Vietnamese heritage. An attorney by day, Kim Luu-Ng helps at the restaurant a couple of nights a week, giving the Spice Table a mom-and-pop vibe. Ng credits Kim for giving him ideas for the menu like frying cauliflower (a vegetable common in Vietnamese cuisine) in beer batter, then serving it with a *nuoc cham*–style dipping sauce made with lime, chile and fish sauce (page 134). She also influenced the range of banh mi that he serves at lunchtime, when the Spice Table functions as a more casual sandwich shop.

Given his affinity for the mash-up cuisine of Singapore, it's not surprising that Ng loves the multiculti offerings of Los Angeles, where taco stands sit next to ramen spots in little strip malls. Ng's personal style of cooking fits right into the city's culinary landscape. As Jonathan Gold says, "His food tastes like L.A."

> **Ng is a startlingly good new chef, reworking the funky, perfumed flavors of his Singaporean heritage with the kind of technique expected from a veteran of Mozza and Daniel.**

THE SPICE TABLE **BRYANT NG**

In Vietnam, cauliflower is traditionally eaten dipped in fish sauce. Ng, too, creates a fish sauce for dipping, but he fries the cauliflower in a spicy beer batter until the florets are tender and the crust is crispy.

FRIED CAULIFLOWER WITH TANGY DIPPING SAUCE

TOTAL *45 min*   **MAKES** *8 first-course servings*

3 tablespoons Asian fish sauce
2 tablespoons fresh lime juice
1 tablespoon sugar
1 garlic clove, minced
1 to 2 Thai chiles, thinly sliced
1½ cups cornstarch
1 cup all-purpose flour
2 teaspoons cayenne pepper
1 teaspoon baking powder
Salt
12 ounces pale lager
1 large egg white
Canola oil, for frying
1 head of cauliflower—halved,
    cored and cut into 1-inch florets
2 tablespoons chopped mint
2 tablespoons very thinly sliced
    jalapeño

PAIR WITH *Crisp sparkling cava:*
NV German Gilabert

1 In a small bowl, whisk the fish sauce with the lime juice, sugar, garlic, Thai chile and 3 tablespoons of water until the sugar dissolves.

2 In a large bowl, whisk the cornstarch with the flour, cayenne, baking powder and 2 teaspoons of salt. Whisk in the beer. In a medium bowl, beat the egg white until stiff peaks form. Using a rubber spatula, fold the beaten egg white into the batter.

3 In a large saucepan, heat 2 inches of canola oil over moderately high heat until it registers 350° on a deep-fry thermometer. Set a rack on a baking sheet. Working in 3 batches, dip the cauliflower florets in the batter and fry until golden, 3 to 5 minutes per batch. Transfer the cauliflower to the rack to drain.

4 In a large serving bowl, toss the fried cauliflower with the mint, jalapeño and a pinch of salt. Serve right away, with the dipping sauce on the side.

134   **FOOD & WINE** AMERICA'S GREATEST NEW COOKS

Ng reinterprets the spicy Thai meat salad called larb *with raw sushi-grade salmon. The result is light, bright and fiery, with heat from two kinds of chile: dried red and fresh Thai.*

SPICY SALMON TARTARE WITH CABBAGE, GREEN BEANS & HERBS

TOTAL *45 min*   **MAKES** *4 first-course servings*

1 tablespoon fresh lime juice
1 tablespoon Asian fish sauce
1 tablespoon palm sugar or light brown sugar
1 cilantro stem, chopped, plus 1 tablespoon finely chopped cilantro leaves
½ teaspoon soy sauce
½ small garlic clove
½ small Thai chile
1 small dried red chile, such as chile de árbol—halved lengthwise, seeded and minced
¼ pound green beans, trimmed
½ cup shredded green cabbage
Salt
¾ pound skinless sushi-quality salmon fillet, cut into ¼-inch dice
1 small shallot, minced
1 scallion, white and light green parts only, thinly sliced
1 tablespoon finely chopped mint
1 tablespoon roasted rice powder (optional; see Note)

PAIR WITH *Zippy, lemony Albariño: 2011 Martín Códax*

1 In a blender, combine the lime juice with the fish sauce, sugar, cilantro stem, soy sauce, garlic, Thai chile and half of the dried red chile. Puree until the dressing is smooth.

2 In a medium pot of salted boiling water, blanch the green beans until crisp-tender, about 4 minutes. Drain and cool under running water; pat dry. Thinly slice the beans on the diagonal. In a medium bowl, toss the sliced beans with the cabbage and 1 teaspoon of the dressing; season with salt.

3 In another medium bowl, toss the salmon with the shallot, scallion, cilantro leaves, mint, rice powder and the remaining dried red chile. Stir in the remaining dressing and season with salt. Spoon the salmon tartare onto plates and serve the green beans and cabbage alongside.

NOTE *Roasted rice powder, known as khao kua pon in Thailand, is available at Asian markets, but you can also make it at home. In a skillet, toast raw white sticky (glutinous) rice over moderately low heat, tossing occasionally, until lightly browned, about 15 minutes. Transfer to a mortar or spice grinder and let cool completely, then grind to a powder. The rice powder can be stored in an airtight container at room temperature for up to 6 months.*

Panko and cornstarch give these juicy chicken wings an irresistibly crisp coating, while curry powder provides a flavor boost. The brilliant idea to include curry in the marinade came from Ng's wife, Kim.

CURRY FRIED CHICKEN WINGS

TOTAL *45 min plus overnight marinating*   **MAKES** *4 to 6 servings*

2 pounds chicken wings, cut into
   2 pieces at the joints
2 tablespoons Madras curry powder
Kosher salt
6 garlic cloves, crushed
¼ cup coconut vinegar (see Note)
   or unseasoned rice vinegar
1 tablespoon Asian fish sauce
1 cup cornstarch
2 large eggs, lightly beaten
2 tablespoons unsweetened
   coconut milk
2 cups all-purpose flour
1 cup panko (Japanese bread
   crumbs), finely crushed
2 teaspoons cayenne pepper
2 teaspoons freshly ground
   white pepper
2 teaspoons freshly ground
   black pepper
Vegetable oil, for frying
Lime wedges, for serving

PAIR WITH *Spiced, red berry–scented Pinot Noir: 2010 Freeman Russian River Valley*

1 In a shallow baking dish, toss the chicken wings with 1 tablespoon of the curry powder and 2 teaspoons of salt; arrange the wings in a single layer. Nestle the garlic around the wings and drizzle the vinegar and fish sauce over them. Cover and refrigerate overnight.

2 Spread the cornstarch in pie plate and season with 1 teaspoon of salt. In another pie plate, whisk the eggs with the coconut milk. In a large bowl, whisk the flour with the panko, cayenne, white and black pepper, 1 teaspoon of salt and the remaining 1 tablespoon of curry powder.

3 Line a baking sheet with wax paper. Working in batches, dredge the wings in the cornstarch and shake off the excess, then dip them in the egg mixture and coat thoroughly with the panko flour. Transfer the wings to the baking sheet.

4 In a large saucepan, heat 2 inches of oil to 350°. Add half of the wings and fry over moderate heat, turning once, until deep golden brown and cooked through, about 8 minutes. Transfer the wings to paper towels to drain and fry the remaining wings. Serve with lime wedges.

NOTE *Coconut vinegar is a low-acid vinegar made from the sap of coconut trees. It is available at health food stores and online.*

Pork satay, a staple among hawkers in Singapore, is typically very sweet. Ng's version, which he marinates in a combination of lemongrass and coconut milk, is more balanced. He also adds extra fennel seeds, making the tender skewered meat even more aromatic.

PORK SATAY

TOTAL *40 min plus overnight marinating*   **MAKES** *4 to 6 servings*

3   large shallots, chopped (¾ cup)

¼   cup unsweetened coconut milk

2   plump fresh lemongrass stalks,
tender inner bulbs only, chopped

1   Fresno chile, chopped

2   Brazil nuts or macadamia nuts,
crushed

1   tablespoon palm sugar or
light brown sugar

1½   teaspoons ground fennel seeds

½   teaspoon crushed red pepper

½   teaspoon freshly ground black
pepper

½   teaspoon shrimp paste
(see Note) or anchovy paste

Kosher salt

1   tablespoon vegetable oil, plus
more for brushing

1½   pounds pork shoulder, cut into
1-by-¼-inch strips

1   teaspoon granulated sugar

Lime wedges, for serving

PAIR WITH *Light, fruit-forward
Dolcetto: 2011 Palmina*

1 In a food processor, combine the shallots, coconut milk, lemongrass, chile, nuts, palm sugar, fennel seeds, crushed red pepper, black pepper, shrimp paste, ½ teaspoon of salt and the 1 tablespoon of oil. Process until a paste forms.

2 In a large bowl, toss the pork strips with the shallot paste, 1 teaspoon of salt and the granulated sugar. Cover with plastic wrap and refrigerate overnight.

3 Soak 12 bamboo skewers in water for at least 30 minutes. Light a grill. Thread the pork onto the skewers, brush with vegetable oil and season with salt. Grill over moderate heat, turning occasionally, until lightly charred and just cooked through, about 10 minutes. Transfer the pork skewers to a platter and serve with lime wedges.

NOTE *Shrimp paste is available at Asian markets.*

At the Spice Table, Ng simmers traditional bone-in catfish steaks in a sweet-savory caramel sauce. The simpler version here calls for easier-to-find catfish fillets, which are just as delicious.

CLAY POT–STYLE CATFISH IN CARAMEL SAUCE

TOTAL *45 min*   **MAKES** *4 to 6 servings*

2 tablespoons vegetable oil, plus more for frying
Two 1-inch pieces of peeled fresh ginger—1 cut into thin matchsticks, 1 cut into 8 thin rounds
2 tablespoons granulated sugar
1½ tablespoons Asian fish sauce
1 tablespoon palm sugar or light brown sugar
½ teaspoon freshly ground black pepper
1 cup plain unsweetened coconut water
6 large shallots, thinly sliced
2 Thai chiles, halved lengthwise
2 garlic cloves, minced
3 scallions, white and light green parts only, cut into 2-inch pieces
Four 8-ounce skinless catfish fillets, halved crosswise
Chopped cilantro, for garnish
Steamed rice, for serving

PAIR WITH *Lightly sweet German Riesling: 2011 Leitz Dragonstone*

1 In a small skillet, heat ¼ inch of oil until shimmering. Add the ginger matchsticks and fry over moderate heat, stirring, until browned and crisp, about 2 minutes. Using a slotted spoon, transfer the fried ginger to paper towels to drain.

2 In a small saucepan, combine the granulated sugar with 1 tablespoon of water. Cook over moderate heat until a deep amber caramel forms, 3 to 4 minutes. Whisk in another 2 tablespoons of water and cook over low heat until the caramel is dissolved, 1 minute. Add the fish sauce, palm sugar, black pepper and ¾ cup of the coconut water and simmer over moderate heat until the caramel sauce is reduced to ½ cup, 3 to 5 minutes.

3 In a large enameled cast-iron casserole, heat the 2 tablespoons of oil until shimmering. Add the ginger rounds, shallots, chiles and garlic and stir-fry over moderately high heat until the shallots are golden, about 3 minutes. Add the caramel sauce and scallions and simmer until the sauce is reduced by half, 3 to 5 minutes. Nestle the catfish fillets in the sauce and cook over moderately high heat, turning once, until caramelized and cooked through, about 6 minutes. Using a spatula, transfer the catfish fillets to a serving platter.

4 Add the remaining ¼ cup of coconut water to the casserole and cook over low heat, scraping up any browned bits from the bottom, until the sauce is hot, about 3 minutes. Spoon the caramel sauce over the catfish. Scatter the fried ginger matchsticks and cilantro over the fish and serve with steamed rice.

This is Ng's twist on a classic seafood pan roast. "I thought, Why not do a soup with oysters?" In place of the usual heavy cream, he enriches the broth with fragrant coconut milk.

OYSTER & CRAB PAN ROAST

TOTAL *45 min*   **MAKES** *6 to 8 servings*

4 tablespoons unsalted butter

3 plump fresh lemongrass stalks— bottom 8 inches only, outer layer removed, stalk cut into 2-inch lengths

2 large shallots, minced

4 garlic cloves, minced

2 Thai chiles, thinly sliced

Salt

½ cup wheat beer or pale lager

4 plum tomatoes, coarsely chopped

4 kaffir lime leaves (see Note)

Three 14½-ounce cans unsweetened coconut milk

½ pound lump crabmeat, picked over

1 dozen oysters, shucked

2 ounces pollack roe or tobiko (flying-fish roe)

2 tablespoons fresh lime juice

PAIR WITH *Aromatic, lively white: 2011 Bedrock Wine Co. Kick Ranch Sauvignon Blanc*

1 In a large saucepan, melt the butter. Add the lemongrass, shallots, garlic, chiles and a generous pinch of salt. Cook over moderately high heat, stirring, until the shallots are softened and just starting to brown, about 2 minutes. Add the beer and boil until evaporated, about 3 minutes. Add the tomatoes and kaffir lime leaves, then crush the tomatoes with a wooden spoon. Simmer over moderately low heat until most of the liquid has evaporated, about 5 minutes. Add the coconut milk and simmer over moderate heat, stirring occasionally, until thickened, about 15 minutes.

2 Add the crabmeat, oysters, pollack roe and lime juice to the saucepan and cook over low heat until warmed through, about 2 minutes. Season with salt. Transfer the pan roast to bowls and serve.

SERVE WITH *Grilled bread and lime wedges.*

NOTE *Kaffir lime leaves, popular in Indonesian, Thai and other Southeast Asian cuisines, are available at specialty food stores and online.*

At the Spice Table, Ng cooks these steaks over almond wood on the satay grill. The anchovies and dry mustard in the marinade add a salty, almost umami-like flavor to the meat; the brown sugar gives it a beautiful crust.

SOUTHEAST ASIAN RIB EYE STEAKS

ACTIVE *20 min*   **TOTAL** *2 hr 30 min*   **MAKES** *4 servings*

Four 1-inch-thick rib eye steaks
    (about 3½ pounds)
Salt
  1 tablespoon plus 1 teaspoon
      dry mustard
  1 tablespoon dark brown sugar
 10 anchovy fillets, minced
  2 teaspoons onion powder
  2 teaspoons garlic powder
  2 teaspoons ground ginger
  2 teaspoons freshly ground
      black pepper
  1 teaspoon freshly ground
      white pepper

PAIR WITH *Ripe, coffee-scented Washington state red: 2009 Buty Rediviva of the Stones*

1 Season the rib eye steaks with salt and let them stand at room temperature for 10 minutes.

2 In a medium bowl, combine the dry mustard and brown sugar with 2 tablespoons of warm water. Stir until the sugar is dissolved, then stir in the remaining ingredients.

3 Spread the paste on both sides of the steaks and refrigerate for 2 hours.

4 Bring the steaks to room temperature. Light a grill or preheat a grill pan. Grill the steaks over moderately high heat for about 3 minutes per side, until they are nicely charred outside and medium-rare within. Let the steaks rest for 5 minutes before serving.

SERVE WITH *Sautéed bok choy.*

The key to this simple cabbage stir-fry is dried shrimp, which add a little bit of funk and a ton of flavor. It's a nostalgic dish for Ng, whose mother used to cook it for him when he was a child.

STIR-FRIED CABBAGE WITH BACON & DRIED SHRIMP

ACTIVE *30 min*   **TOTAL** *1 hr*   **MAKES** *4 to 6 servings*

1 tablespoon dried shrimp
(about 12 small shrimp; see Note)
2 slices of thick-cut bacon (about
2 ounces), cut into ½-inch pieces
3 garlic cloves, thinly sliced
2 pounds green or napa cabbage,
cored and cut into 1-inch pieces
2 teaspoons sugar
Kosher salt and freshly ground
black pepper

1 In a small bowl, soak the shrimp in water for 30 minutes. Drain and coarsely chop the shrimp. In a mortar, pound the shrimp until crumbled.

2 In a wok or large skillet, stir-fry the bacon over moderate heat until browned, about 6 minutes. Add the garlic and dried shrimp and stir-fry until fragrant, 1 minute. Add the cabbage, sugar and a generous pinch each of salt and pepper and stir-fry until the cabbage starts to soften, about 3 minutes. Add ¼ cup of water and cook, stirring occasionally, until the cabbage is crisp-tender, about 10 minutes. Season the cabbage with salt and pepper and serve.

NOTE *Dried shrimp are available at Asian markets.*

Bok choy is usually stir-fried, but Ng char-grills it until it's smoky, tops it with deeply savory braised shiitake mushrooms, then drizzles the dish with a ginger-scented oyster sauce.

GRILLED BOK CHOY WITH BRAISED MUSHROOMS

ACTIVE *1 hr*   **TOTAL** *2 hr plus overnight soaking*   **MAKES** *4 servings*

2½ ounces dried shiitake mushrooms (about 5 cups)

3 tablespoons canola oil, plus more for brushing

One 1-inch piece of peeled fresh ginger—½ inch smashed, ½ inch cut into thin matchsticks

½ ounce rock sugar, crushed, or 1 tablespoon granulated sugar

1 scallion, cut into 3-inch lengths

2 cups plus 2 tablespoons chicken stock or low-sodium broth

¼ cup plus 1 tablespoon oyster sauce

Kosher salt

1 teaspoon unaged whiskey or other grain alcohol

1 pound bok choy, quartered lengthwise

1 In a large bowl, cover the shiitake with water and let soak overnight at room temperature. Drain the mushrooms and discard the stems.

2 In a large saucepan, heat 2 tablespoons of the oil until shimmering. Add the smashed ginger, sugar and scallion and cook over moderate heat, stirring, until the sugar dissolves and starts to caramelize, 4 to 5 minutes. Add the mushrooms and the 2 cups of chicken stock and bring to a boil. Cover partially and simmer over low heat, stirring occasionally, until the mushrooms are tender and most of the stock has evaporated, about 1 hour and 15 minutes. Stir in the 1 tablespoon of oyster sauce and season the braised mushrooms with salt.

3 Meanwhile, in a small saucepan, heat the remaining 1 tablespoon of oil until shimmering. Add the ginger matchsticks and cook over moderately high heat, stirring, until lightly golden, 1 minute. Add the whiskey and cook for 30 seconds. Add the remaining 2 tablespoons of chicken stock and ¼ cup of oyster sauce and simmer over moderately low heat until thickened, about 5 minutes. Keep the ginger-oyster sauce warm.

4 In a large pot of salted boiling water, blanch the bok choy until crisp-tender, about 2 minutes. Drain and cool under running water; pat dry.

5 Light a grill or preheat a grill pan. Brush the bok choy with oil and grill over high heat, turning, until lightly charred, about 5 minutes. Transfer to plates or a platter and top with the mushrooms. Drizzle the ginger-oyster sauce over the bok choy and mushrooms and serve.

MAKE AHEAD *The braised mushrooms and ginger-oyster sauce can be refrigerated separately overnight. Reheat gently before serving.*

This dreamy custard is supersilky and astonishingly simple to make. The secret: It firms up in a couple of hours with lime juice instead of the usual eggs or gelatin.

KAFFIR LIME CUSTARDS

TOTAL *30 min plus 2 hr chilling*   **MAKES** *8 servings*

3½ cups heavy cream
1 cup sugar
2 kaffir lime leaves (see Note)
½ cup plus 2 tablespoons fresh
   lime juice
2 teaspoons finely grated lime zest
¼ teaspoon salt
Sweetened whipped cream,
   quartered lychees, chopped mint
   and sea salt, for garnish

1 In a medium saucepan, combine the cream with the sugar and kaffir lime leaves and bring to a simmer. Cook over moderately low heat, stirring occasionally, until the cream is slightly reduced, about 15 minutes.

2 Whisk the lime juice into the hot cream. Strain the cream through a fine sieve set over a measuring cup. Stir in the lime zest and salt. Pour the cream into eight 6-ounce glasses and refrigerate for at least 2 hours, until chilled and set. Top the custards with whipped cream, garnish with lychees, mint and sea salt and serve right away.

NOTE *Kaffir lime leaves, popular in Indonesian, Thai and other Southeast Asian cuisines, are available at specialty food stores and online.*

MAKE AHEAD *The custards can be refrigerated overnight. Garnish just before serving.*

SARAH SIMMONS

CHEF / FOUNDER • CITY GRIT • NEW YORK CITY

for someone who didn't go to culinary school, has never run a restaurant and would probably not impress a master like Jacques Pépin with her kitchen techniques, Sarah Simmons has made a big impression on the food world. She's the visionary behind one of the most exciting culinary happenings in Manhattan: City Grit, a pop-up restaurant (or "culinary salon," as Simmons calls it) in a renovated schoolhouse with a rotating list of guest chefs and themes that change from night to night. The tables are communal, the furnishings are all for sale and the vibe is more like a boisterous dinner party than a restaurant. "I love the unpredictability of City Grit," says *Food & Wine* restaurant editor Kate Krader. "Every time you go, it's a different chef, and because of the set menu, you try dishes you wouldn't necessarily order. It's like gambling with your dinner, in the best possible way."

Simmons represents a new breed of food-world star: the home cook and chef groupie who manages to turn semipro. Just a few years ago, the North Carolina native was working in digital marketing in Manhattan and hosting elaborate dinner parties at night. "I'd lure people in by saying, 'Come over, I'll make grits for you!'" she recalls. "But it was really just a way for me to improve as a cook." Using her social networking savvy, Simmons won F&W's Home Cook Superstar contest in 2010. "Winning gave me confidence to quit my job and move into the food world," Simmons says. "But I felt like my cooking skills weren't good enough." She embarked on a series of apprenticeships, with Hugh Acheson at Atlanta's Empire State South and Michael Anthony at New York City's Gramercy Tavern.

Working in great restaurant kitchens taught Simmons that she "didn't want to be a regular chef who had to cook the same thing over and over." So she came up with the idea for City Grit, which matches her love of cooking with her most significant talent: connecting people through the force of her enthusiasm. "She's like the ultimate superfan," says Krader. "And that really flatters chefs, who then want to be a part of what she's doing." Simmons has attracted top talent to her kitchen, including Paul Qui of Uchiko in Austin and John Currence of City Grocery in Oxford, Mississippi. "City Grit hits all the high points of what dining ought to be—sharing, interacting, community," says Currence. "Just the way that the tables are set up forces people to interact, instead of being cliquey with their friends."

Even when guest chefs are running the show, Simmons is in the kitchen helping out. When Simmons herself cooks at City Grit, she draws inspiration from her childhood in Fayetteville, North Carolina. Her food is Southern-inspired, but with some playful tweaks. For instance, she uses Parmesan instead of the usual cheddar in her cheesy grits (page 172). "I've come up with over 100 recipes for grits," she says. "It's my safe, happy-time food." She also creates unique menus for themed nights at City Grit; for a Tour of the Five Boroughs dinner, she made short ribs braised in Brooklyn Brewery's chocolate stout (page 166); for a Southern Small Plates night, she topped seared scallops with a sweet-savory bacon marmalade (page 164).

Just a few years ago Simmons couldn't have imagined cooking a five-course dinner for 85, or working alongside some of her chef heroes—but now she's doing that a few times a month. "When I moved to New York eight years ago, I was miserable," she recalls. "Now I get standing ovations at dinner and emails from chefs who want to come cook here."

> "City Grit really hits all the high points of what dining ought to be: sharing, interacting, community. And Sarah is right there, magnificently in the middle of everything.

For a New York City–inspired dinner at City Grit, Simmons created this crisp salad to represent Staten Island. "In my mind," she says, "that borough is all Italian. Or at least I think it is." Dried cherries, toasted pine nuts, endive and radicchio give the salad sweet, savory and bitter flavors.

SHAVED-FENNEL SALAD WITH ANCHOVY VINAIGRETTE

TOTAL *30 min*   **MAKES** *4 to 6 servings*

½ cup pine nuts
2 tablespoons red wine vinegar
2 tablespoons minced shallot
3 anchovy fillets, chopped
1 teaspoon Dijon mustard
1 garlic clove, minced
⅓ cup extra-virgin olive oil
Salt and freshly ground pepper
2 large fennel bulbs—halved lengthwise, cored and very thinly sliced crosswise
1 Belgian endive—halved lengthwise, cored and thinly sliced crosswise
1 small head of radicchio (6 ounces)—halved lengthwise, cored and thinly sliced crosswise
½ cup dried cherries
Freshly shaved Parmigiano-Reggiano cheese, for garnish

1 In a small skillet, toast the pine nuts over moderate heat, shaking the pan, until the nuts are lightly golden, about 4 minutes.

2 In a blender, combine the vinegar with the shallot, anchovies, mustard and garlic and puree until smooth. With the blender on, drizzle in the olive oil until the vinaigrette is emulsified. Season with salt and pepper.

3 In a large bowl, toss the fennel slices with the endive and radicchio. Add the anchovy vinaigrette, pine nuts and cherries and toss to coat. Season the salad with salt and pepper, garnish with cheese shavings and serve right away.

This is Simmons's completely inauthentic take on Chinese peanut noodles. Made with soba noodles and Thai pantry staples (red curry paste, coconut milk, chile and cilantro), it's lighter, brighter and spicier than the original.

SPICY SOBA NOODLE SALAD WITH THAI-STYLE PEANUT DRESSING

TOTAL *50 min*   **MAKES** *6 first-course servings*

1½ tablespoons vegetable oil
¼ cup finely chopped Vidalia or other sweet onion
1 jalapeño, seeded and minced
2 garlic cloves, minced
1 tablespoon minced peeled fresh ginger
¼ cup creamy peanut butter
1½ tablespoons Thai red curry paste
½ cup unsweetened coconut milk
⅓ cup chicken stock or low-sodium broth
1 tablespoon soy sauce
2 teaspoons sugar
2 tablespoons fresh lime juice
Salt
1 pound dried soba noodles
1 cup finely julienned carrots
1 cup finely julienned cucumber
Finely grated lime zest and chopped cilantro, for garnish

1 In a medium saucepan, heat 1 tablespoon of the oil until shimmering. Add the onion and cook over moderate heat, stirring occasionally, until softened and just starting to brown, about 5 minutes. Add the jalapeño, garlic and ginger and cook until fragrant, 1 minute. Add the peanut butter and red curry paste and cook over moderately low heat, stirring, until smooth, about 2 minutes. Whisk in the coconut milk, chicken stock, soy sauce and sugar and simmer until thickened slightly, about 3 minutes. Remove from the heat. Whisk in the lime juice and season with salt; let cool completely.

2 Meanwhile, in a large pot of salted boiling water, cook the soba noodles until al dente, about 5 minutes. Drain and rinse under cold running water until cooled. Shake out the excess water and blot the soba dry. Transfer the noodles to a large bowl and toss with the remaining ½ tablespoon of oil. Add the spicy peanut dressing and toss well to coat thoroughly. Add the carrots and cucumber and toss again. Garnish the soba with the lime zest and cilantro and serve.

MAKE AHEAD *The peanut dressing can be refrigerated for up to 2 days.*

Simmons layers this rich white lasagna with cheddar cheese and pesto instead of the usual mozzarella, ricotta and tomato sauce. She tops the dish with a generous amount of Parmesan, which creates a beautiful crust with delectable, crispy edges as it bakes.

PESTO & CHEDDAR LASAGNA

ACTIVE *1 hr* **TOTAL** *2 hr 15 min* **MAKES** *8 servings*

¼ cup pine nuts

4 cups packed basil leaves

2 garlic cloves, chopped

2 tablespoons extra-virgin olive oil

Salt and freshly ground pepper

1½ sticks unsalted butter, plus more for greasing

¾ cup all-purpose flour

6 cups whole milk, warmed

Pinch of freshly grated nutmeg

1½ pounds dried lasagna noodles

1 pound sharp white cheddar cheese, shredded

½ cup freshly grated Parmigiano-Reggiano cheese

PAIR WITH *Fruit-forward, unoaked Chardonnay: 2010 Foxglove*

1 In a small skillet, toast the pine nuts over moderate heat until lightly golden, about 4 minutes; let cool. In a food processor, pulse the basil with the pine nuts and garlic until finely chopped. With the machine on, drizzle in the olive oil and process until a paste forms. Season the pesto with salt and pepper.

2 In a medium saucepan, melt the 1½ sticks of butter over moderate heat. Whisk in the flour to make a paste and cook until bubbling, about 3 minutes. Gradually whisk in the milk until smooth and bring to a boil. Simmer over moderately low heat, whisking, until the sauce is thick and no floury taste remains, about 7 minutes. Stir in the pesto and nutmeg and season with salt and pepper. Cover and remove from the heat.

3 Preheat the oven to 400° and butter a 9-by-13-inch ceramic baking dish. In a large pot of salted boiling water, cook the lasagna noodles until al dente, 6 to 7 minutes. Drain the noodles and transfer to a baking sheet.

4 Spread ⅓ cup of the pesto sauce in the prepared baking dish. Arrange a single layer of the noodles over the sauce. Top with one-fourth of the remaining sauce and one-third of the cheddar. Repeat this layering twice, then top with a final layer of noodles and the remaining sauce. Sprinkle the Parmigiano on top.

5 Cover the lasagna with aluminum foil and bake for about 30 minutes, until heated through. Uncover and bake for 15 to 20 minutes longer, until the top is golden in spots. Cover loosely and let rest for 15 minutes before serving.

MAKE AHEAD *The unbaked lasagna can be refrigerated overnight. Bring to room temperature before baking.*

Simmons tops scallops with a sweet-and-spicy bacon-onion marmalade (which she also likes to spoon on grits). The creamy carrot puree served alongside gets its subtle heat from harissa, a North African chile paste.

SEARED SCALLOPS WITH BACON MARMALADE

TOTAL *1 hr 15 min*   **MAKES** *4 servings*

½ pound cold thick-cut bacon, cut into ¼-inch dice
1 onion, finely diced
2 tablespoons light brown sugar
Cayenne pepper
Kosher salt and freshly ground black pepper
1 pound carrots, cut into ½-inch pieces
2 tablespoons unsalted butter
2 teaspoons harissa (see Note)
¼ cup heavy cream
16 large sea scallops (about 1½ pounds)
1 tablespoon extra-virgin olive oil

PAIR WITH *Minerally, full-bodied white Burgundy: 2010 Domaine Roulot Bourgogne Blanc*

1 In a medium cast-iron skillet, cook the bacon over moderate heat, stirring occasionally, until crisp, 6 to 7 minutes. Using a slotted spoon, transfer the bacon to a plate. Pour off all but 2 tablespoons of the bacon fat. Add the onion to the skillet and cook over moderately low heat, stirring occasionally, until soft and golden, about 25 minutes. Add the sugar and cook until the sugar is dissolved and the onions are glazed, about 2 minutes. Return the bacon to the skillet; season with cayenne pepper, salt and black pepper. Keep the bacon marmalade warm.

2 In a medium saucepan of salted boiling water, cook the carrots until tender, 5 to 7 minutes. Drain well. In a food processor, combine the carrots with the butter and harissa and puree until smooth. Add the cream and pulse until incorporated. Season with salt and black pepper. Scrape the carrot-harissa puree into the saucepan; keep warm over very low heat.

3 Season the scallops with salt and black pepper. In a large skillet, heat the olive oil until shimmering. Add the scallops and cook over moderately high heat until browned on the bottom, about 2 minutes. Turn the scallops and cook until just opaque throughout, about 1 minute longer. Transfer the scallops to plates and top with the bacon marmalade. Serve the carrot-harissa puree alongside.

NOTE *Harissa is a North African chile paste. It is available in jars and tubes at specialty food shops.*

MAKE AHEAD *The bacon marmalade and carrot-harissa puree can be refrigerated separately overnight.*

Braising short ribs in beer makes them supertender and adds a slight bitter note. Simmons cooks her ribs in Brooklyn Brewery Black Chocolate Stout, but you can use any dark beer.

STOUT-BRAISED SHORT RIBS

ACTIVE *1 hr*   **TOTAL** *3 hr 20 min*   **MAKES** *6 servings*

2 tablespoons canola oil
6 boneless short ribs
   (10 to 12 ounces each)
Kosher salt and freshly ground pepper
1 onion, thinly sliced
1 large carrot, thinly sliced
3 cups beef stock or low-
   sodium broth
2 cups chocolate stout or
   other dark beer
Creamy Parmesan Grits (page 172),
   for serving

PAIR WITH *Spiced, berry-rich Merlot: 2009 Covey Run*

1 Preheat the oven to 325°. In a large enameled cast-iron casserole, heat the oil until shimmering. Season the short ribs with salt and pepper and add 3 of them to the casserole. Cook over moderate heat, turning, until well browned all over, about 10 minutes. Transfer to a plate and repeat with the remaining ribs.

2 Pour off all but 2 tablespoons of the fat from the casserole. Add the onion and carrot and cook over moderate heat, stirring occasionally, until the vegetables are softened, about 8 minutes. Add the beef stock and beer and bring to a boil. Return the ribs to the casserole, cover and braise in the oven for about 2 hours, until the meat is very tender.

3 Transfer the ribs to a platter and tent with foil. Using a slotted spoon, transfer the vegetables to a blender. Strain the sauce into a heatproof measuring cup and skim off the fat. Add the sauce to the blender and puree until smooth. Return

the sauce to the casserole and boil until reduced to 3 cups, about 8 minutes. Season with salt and pepper. Return the short ribs to the sauce and simmer over low heat until they are warmed through. Serve the ribs with the grits.

MAKE AHEAD *The short ribs can be refrigerated in the sauce for up to 3 days.*

Vidalia onion soufflé was a fixture at Thanksgiving and Christmas meals in Simmons's home when she was growing up in Fayetteville, North Carolina. This version—lighter and airier than the one her mother makes—can be prepared in individual gratin dishes or in one big baking dish.

VIDALIA ONION SOUFFLÉS

ACTIVE *30 min*   **TOTAL** *1 hr 45 min*   **MAKES** *8 servings*

1   stick unsalted butter, plus more for greasing

4   pounds Vidalia or other sweet onions, thinly sliced

Salt

3   tablespoons all-purpose flour

2   teaspoons baking powder

6   large eggs

2   cups heavy cream

¾   cup freshly grated Parmigiano-Reggiano cheese

1 In a very large skillet, melt the stick of butter over moderately low heat. Add the onions and a generous pinch of salt and cook, stirring occasionally, until soft and golden, about 40 minutes. Let the onions cool completely.

2 Preheat the oven to 350° and butter eight 5½-inch gratin dishes (see Note). In a small bowl, whisk the flour with the baking powder and 1 teaspoon of salt. In a large bowl, beat the eggs with the cream and grated cheese. Whisk in the dry ingredients until incorporated, then fold in the onions. Spoon the soufflé mixture into the prepared gratin dishes and bake for about 20 minutes, until set and golden on top. Serve right away.

NOTE *The soufflé mixture can also be baked in a buttered 9-by-13-inch glass or ceramic baking dish for 45 minutes.*

"I've been making collards this way ever since I can remember," Simmons says. *She gives the greens a double dose of smokiness with bacon and paprika and adds jalapeño for a good kick of heat.*

SMOKY COLLARD GREENS

ACTIVE *30 min*   **TOTAL** *2 hr*   **MAKES** *6 to 8 servings*

One ½-pound piece of meaty
    slab bacon
1 jalapeño, halved lengthwise
½ teaspoon garlic powder
Kosher salt and freshly ground pepper
4 tablespoons unsalted butter
1 tablespoon seasoned salt,
    such as Lawry's
¼ teaspoon smoked paprika
3 pounds collard greens,
    stems discarded, leaves cut
    into 1-inch strips

1 In a large pot, cook the bacon over moderately high heat, turning, until it is golden all over, about 4 minutes. Add 3½ quarts of water and bring to a boil. Add the jalapeño, garlic powder, 2 teaspoons of kosher salt and ½ teaspoon of pepper and simmer over low heat until the bacon is fork-tender, about 45 minutes.

2 Bring the broth to a vigorous boil. Stir in the butter, seasoned salt and smoked paprika. Add large handfuls of the collards at a time, allowing each batch to wilt slightly before adding more. Return the broth to a boil. Reduce the heat and simmer the collards over moderate heat, stirring occasionally, until they are tender, about 30 minutes.

3 Discard the jalapeño. Transfer the bacon to a plate, then cut off and discard the skin and fat. Using 2 forks, shred the meat and return it to the pot. Using tongs, transfer the collards and bacon to bowls. Spoon some of the broth over the greens and serve.

MAKE AHEAD *The collards can be refrigerated in their cooking liquid for up to 4 days.*

Simmons, a self-described grits fanatic, has created over 100 recipes for grits, including variations with miso, brown butter and roasted garlic. Here she adds Parmesan, turning the Southern breakfast staple into an elegant side to serve with her short ribs (page 166) or alongside pork tenderloin.

CREAMY PARMESAN GRITS

TOTAL *40 min* **MAKES** *4 to 6 servings*

3 tablespoons unsalted butter
Kosher salt
1 cup stone-ground grits
2 tablespoons all-purpose flour
1 cup low-fat milk
¾ cup freshly grated Parmigiano-
     Reggiano cheese (3 ounces)
Freshly ground pepper

1 In a medium saucepan, bring 3½ cups of water to a boil with 1 tablespoon of the butter. Add a generous pinch of salt and gradually whisk in the grits. Cook over moderately low heat, whisking often, until the grits are thick and just tender, about 30 minutes.

2 Meanwhile, in another medium saucepan, melt the remaining 2 tablespoons of butter. Whisk in the flour, and when it is bubbling, gradually whisk in the milk. Cook over moderate heat, whisking frequently, until thickened and no floury taste remains, 8 to 10 minutes. Stir in the grated cheese and cook until just melted, about 2 minutes.

3 Using a rubber spatula, fold the Parmesan sauce into the grits and season with salt and pepper. Serve right away.

According to legend, this sweet, brioche-like bread was invented by 18th-century baker Sally Lunn in England, then brought over to the Southern colonies. Though it's traditionally baked into buns and spread with clotted cream, Simmons prepares the bread in a tube pan and serves it with butter or pimento cheese.

SALLY LUNN BREAD

ACTIVE *40 min*   **TOTAL** *4 hr 45 min*   **MAKES** *one 10-inch round loaf*

1½ sticks unsalted butter, plus more for greasing
1 cup milk
3 large eggs, separated
One ¼-ounce package active dry yeast
4 cups all-purpose flour
3 tablespoons sugar
2 teaspoons salt

1 In a small saucepan, melt the 1½ sticks of butter in the milk over low heat. Pour the mixture into a medium bowl and let cool slightly, then whisk in the egg yolks. Whisk in the yeast and let stand until foamy, about 5 minutes.

2 In a large bowl, whisk the flour with the sugar and salt. Stir in the milk mixture until a very wet dough forms. In another large bowl, using a handheld electric mixer, beat the egg whites until stiff peaks form, about 2 minutes. Using a rubber spatula, fold the egg whites into the dough until incorporated. Scrape the dough into a very large greased bowl. Using your hands, shape the dough into a round loaf. Cover loosely with plastic wrap and let the dough rise in a warm place until doubled in bulk, about 2 hours.

3 Butter a 10-inch tube pan. Using your hands, punch the dough down and tear an opening in the center of the dough. Transfer the dough to the prepared pan, inserting the tube into the hole in the

dough. Gently pat the dough to the sides of the pan. Cover loosely with plastic wrap and let rise in a warm place until nearly doubled in bulk, about 1 hour.

4 Preheat the oven to 325°. Bake the bread in the center of the oven for 25 minutes, until a crust is just starting to form. Increase the oven temperature to 375° and bake for 20 to 25 minutes longer, until the bread is golden and crusty. Let cool in the pan for 10 minutes. Remove the bread from the pan, cut into slices and serve warm.

MAKE AHEAD *The bread can be wrapped in plastic and kept at room temperature overnight.*

Simmons came up with these moist, chewy blondies when she was left with extra caramel after a City Grit event. The little bit of orange zest is lovely with the sweet-salty caramel.

CITRUS-CARAMEL BLONDIES

ACTIVE *25 min*   **TOTAL** *1 hr 10 min plus cooling*   **MAKES** *16 bars*

CARAMEL
- ¼ cup granulated sugar
- 3 tablespoons heavy cream
- 1 tablespoon cold unsalted butter
- ½ teaspoon Maldon sea salt (see Note)

BLONDIES
- 1 cup all-purpose flour
- 1 teaspoon kosher salt
- ½ teaspoon baking powder
- 1 stick unsalted butter, melted
- 1 cup packed light brown sugar
- 2 large eggs
- ½ teaspoon finely grated orange zest

1 MAKE THE CARAMEL In a small saucepan, combine the granulated sugar with 1 tablespoon of water and bring to a boil. Using a wet pastry brush, wash down any crystals on the side of the pan. Boil the syrup over moderately high heat until a deep amber caramel forms, about 5 minutes. Remove from the heat and immediately whisk in the cream, butter and Maldon sea salt. Let the caramel cool to room temperature.

2 MAKE THE BLONDIES Preheat the oven to 350°. Spray an 8-inch square metal baking pan with nonstick cooking spray and line the pan with parchment paper, allowing 1 inch of overhang on 2 opposite sides; spray the paper. In a small bowl, whisk the flour with the kosher salt and baking powder. In a medium bowl, whisk the butter with the brown sugar until combined, then whisk in the eggs and orange zest. Add the flour mixture and stir until just incorporated.

3 Spread the batter in the prepared pan in an even layer. Drizzle the caramel over the top, then swirl it decoratively using a toothpick. Bake the blondie for 25 to 30 minutes, until it is golden on top and a toothpick inserted in the center comes out with a few moist crumbs attached. Let cool completely. Lift the blondie out by the overhanging parchment and peel off the paper. Cut into bars and serve.

NOTE *Maldon sea salt has a great crunch and a remarkably subtle, briny flavor. It is available at most grocery stores and online.*

MAKE AHEAD *The blondies can be stored in an airtight container at room temperature for up to 3 days.*

JUSTIN SMILLIE

CHEF • IL BUCO ALIMENTARI E VINERIA • NEW YORK CITY

plenty of chefs are committed to finding the best-quality ingredients, but how many have been fired for their devotion to pristine produce? That's what happened to chef Justin Smillie, who was axed by the owner of a Manhattan restaurant for spending too much money at the farmers' market. "It's difficult to find a restaurant owner who shares my value system and goals," says Smillie. Now, as chef at New York City's Il Buco Alimentari e Vineria, a combination Italian grocery–wine bar–restaurant–*salumeria*–bakery, he doesn't have that problem. In Donna Lennard, the restaurant's Italophile owner, Smillie has found an enlightened patron who shares his commitment to making innovative, modern food with super-high-quality ingredients. "Justin was able to fulfill Donna's vision; he listened to her and applied his technique, ideas and passion," says chef Jonathan Waxman, who mentored Smillie for six years at Manhattan's Barbuto and the now-closed Washington Park. "He's taken an Italian sensibility and coupled it with American spirit and ingredients. He's done an amazing job at that."

Smillie's first restaurant job as a teenager was at a New Jersey seafood spot where he boiled crabs. He went to culinary school briefly, then worked in top kitchens throughout New York City, including Mercer Kitchen, Gramercy Tavern and Barbuto. With Waxman, a pioneer of seasonal, Cal-Ital cooking, Smillie got a first-rate education in simplicity. "Chefs often want to use everything in their toolbox to make food glorious and wonderful," Waxman says. "Eventually, Justin got that sometimes glorious and wonderful is really just pure and simple."

After a short tenure at a forgettable, now-defunct gastropub in Manhattan—the one whose owner booted him for spending too much at the farmers' market—Smillie connected with Donna Lennard, who started the rustic, romantic trattoria Il Buco on Bond Street in 1994. Her second place, Il Buco Alimentari e Vineria, maintains the casually chic feel of the original, but expands in scope. In front, the market (the *alimentari*) sells meticulously selected staples like small-batch olive oils, aged cheeses, house-baked breads and incredible *salumi,* much of it from a custom kitchen and aging room in the basement. In the back is the wine-centric restaurant (the *vineria*) with a rotisserie and wood-burning oven, where Smillie cooks.

With all of these incredible provisions on hand, as well as top produce and meat from around the region, Smillie creates Italian dishes that seem elemental but require an enormous amount of time and technique. His signature short ribs, for instance, undergo a two-day preparation of brining, rubbing and spit-roasting before a final crisping in the wood-fired oven. He then garnishes the roast with green olives, walnut, celery, grated horseradish and the southern Italian anchovy sauce called *colatura.* But even his simpler dishes have small, surprising touches. Combining sugar snap peas with ricotta isn't unusual, but Smillie tops them with a savory kasha and pine nut granola (page 184). "I wanted to add something earthy and crunchy, but not just straight-up nuts—everyone does that," he says. Bagna cauda, a warm anchovy–olive oil sauce, is typically used as a dip for raw vegetables; Smillie instead dresses spinach with the pungent sauce, creating a punchy, lusty salad (page 186).

Smillie says his food is about "bold, clean flavors" and the quality of the ingredients, but his skill and talent are what make his cooking truly transformative.

> **Justin has taken an Italian sensibility and coupled it with American spirit and super-high-quality ingredients. He has done a really amazing job at that.**

At Il Buco Alimentari e Vineria, Smillie goes through 60 cases of artichokes a week to keep up with the demand for this dish. He fries the artichokes until the edges are crispy, then tosses them with lemon and orange zest and smoky-hot crushed Aleppo pepper.

FRIED ARTICHOKES WITH CITRUS & PARSLEY

TOTAL *40 min*   **MAKES** *4 first-course servings*

4 large artichokes
½ lemon
Vegetable oil, for frying
2 tablespoons finely chopped parsley
1 teaspoon finely grated lemon zest
1 teaspoon finely grated orange zest
½ teaspoon Aleppo pepper (see Note)
Maldon sea salt

1 Working with 1 artichoke at a time, using a serrated bread knife, trim off all but 2 inches of the leaves. Pull off and discard the dark green outer leaves, then peel and trim the bottom and the stem. Quarter the artichoke and scrape out the hairy choke. Rub the artichoke quarters all over with the lemon half, squeeze the extra lemon juice into a small bowl of water and add the quartered artichoke to the lemon water. Repeat with the remaining artichokes.

2 In a medium saucepan of salted boiling water, blanch the artichokes until they are crisp-tender, about 3 minutes. Drain, transfer to a plate and pat dry.

3 In a medium saucepan, heat 1 inch of oil to 350°. Fry the artichokes until golden and crisp, 3 to 5 minutes. Transfer to paper towels to drain.

4 In a medium bowl, toss the artichokes with the parsley, lemon zest, orange zest and Aleppo pepper. Season with Maldon sea salt and serve right away.

NOTE *Aleppo pepper is a moderately hot crushed dried chile from Turkey and Syria. It is available at gourmet markets and penzeys.com.*

"Everyone adds nuts to salad, but I wanted to do something different," says Smillie. He tops crisp snap peas with a savory granola that includes pine nuts and kasha. Ricotta adds another layer of texture; Smillie makes his own cheese at the restaurant, but good-quality store-bought fresh ricotta is also delicious.

SUGAR SNAP PEA SALAD WITH PINE NUT–KASHA GRANOLA & RICOTTA

ACTIVE *25 min*   **TOTAL** *50 min plus cooling*   **MAKES** *8 first-course servings*

GRANOLA

2¼ cups rolled oats
⅔ cup kasha
    (roasted buckwheat groats)
½ cup flaxseeds
½ cup pine nuts
⅓ cup extra-virgin olive oil
⅓ cup pure maple syrup
¼ cup fresh orange juice
2 teaspoons kosher salt
1½ teaspoons sugar

SALAD

1 pound sugar snap peas
1½ tablespoons fresh lemon juice
1½ tablespoons extra-virgin olive oil,
    plus more for drizzling
Maldon sea salt, kosher salt and
    freshly ground pepper
1 pound fresh ricotta cheese
Chopped mint, for garnish

1 **MAKE THE GRANOLA** Preheat the oven to 325° and line a rimmed baking sheet with parchment paper. In a large bowl, toss the oats with the kasha, flaxseeds and pine nuts. Add the remaining granola ingredients and toss until thoroughly coated, then spread on the prepared baking sheet.

2 Bake the granola in the center of the oven for 30 to 35 minutes, stirring every 10 minutes, until golden and nearly dry. Turn off the oven and prop the door open halfway; let the granola cool in the oven, stirring occasionally.

3 **MAKE THE SALAD** In a medium saucepan of salted boiling water, simmer the snap peas until bright green and crisp-tender, about 1 minute. Drain and cool the snap peas under running water, pat dry and halve them lengthwise. In a medium bowl, toss the snap peas with the lemon juice and 1½ tablespoons of olive oil, then season with Maldon sea salt and pepper.

4 In another medium bowl, whisk the ricotta until smooth and season with kosher salt and pepper. Spoon the ricotta onto plates and top with the snap peas. Sprinkle some of the granola on the peas and garnish with a drizzle of olive oil and chopped mint. Serve right away.

MAKE AHEAD *This recipe makes 5 cups of granola, which can be stored in an airtight container for up to 3 weeks.*

In the Piedmont region of Italy, the warm anchovy–olive oil sauce called bagna cauda is typically served as a dip for vegetables. Here, Smillie turns it into a warm dressing for baby spinach, adding fresh bread crumbs for crunch.

SPINACH SALAD WITH BAGNA CAUDA DRESSING

ACTIVE *20 min*   **TOTAL** *40 min*   **MAKES** *6 to 8 servings*

4 tablespoons unsalted butter
5 anchovies, finely chopped
¼ cup extra-virgin olive oil
2 tablespoons red wine vinegar
1 tablespoon fresh lemon juice, plus lemon wedges for serving
3 thyme sprigs
Kosher salt and freshly ground pepper
¼ cup coarse dry bread crumbs (see Note)
10 ounces baby spinach
Freshly shaved Parmigiano-Reggiano cheese, for garnish

1 In a small saucepan, melt the butter over moderate heat until foaming. Add the anchovies and cook over moderately low heat until dissolved, about 2 minutes. Remove from the heat and whisk in the olive oil, vinegar and lemon juice. Add the thyme sprigs and let steep for 20 minutes. Discard the thyme and season the dressing with salt and pepper.

2 Meanwhile, in a small skillet, toast the bread crumbs over moderate heat, tossing, until golden, about 4 minutes. Let the bread crumbs cool.

3 In a large bowl, toss the spinach with half of the dressing and bread crumbs and season with salt and pepper. Transfer the salad to plates or a platter and top with the remaining bread crumbs and the shaved Parmigiano-Reggiano. Pass the remaining dressing at the table and serve with lemon wedges.

NOTE *To make bread crumbs, tear 2 slices of day-old white bread into pieces, spread on a baking sheet and toast in a 300° oven until dried but not browned, about 10 minutes. Transfer to a food processor and pulse until coarse crumbs form.*

MAKE AHEAD *The bagna cauda dressing can be refrigerated overnight. Warm gently before using.*

Ramps, the ephemeral wild onions that chefs love and which appear only in the spring, give this pasta a lovely garlic flavor. When ramps aren't in season, Smillie uses elephant garlic—the bulb, stem and flowers. Scallions also make a good substitute.

SPAGHETTI WITH RAMPS, CHILES & TWO CHEESES

TOTAL *30 min* **MAKES** *6 servings*

1 *pound spaghetti*

3 *tablespoons unsalted butter*

¼ *cup extra-virgin olive oil*

½ *pound ramps or medium scallions, thinly sliced*

Kosher salt and freshly ground pepper

2 or 3 Thai chiles, thinly sliced

2 *dried red chiles such as Calabrian, crumbled*

2 *tablespoons fresh lemon juice*

¼ *cup freshly grated Pecorino Romano cheese*

¼ *cup freshly grated Parmigiano-Reggiano cheese, plus more for serving*

PAIR WITH *Zesty, full-bodied Sicilian white: 2011 Occhipinti SP68 Bianco*

1 In a large saucepan of salted boiling water, cook the spaghetti until al dente. Drain the pasta, reserving 1 cup of the cooking water.

2 Meanwhile, in a large skillet, melt the butter in the olive oil. Add the ramps and a generous pinch each of salt and pepper and cook over moderately high heat, stirring, until just wilted, about 3 minutes. Add the fresh and dried chiles and cook for 30 seconds. Stir in the lemon juice and the ¼ cup each of pecorino and Parmigiano cheese.

3 Add the spaghetti to the skillet along with the reserved cooking water and cook over moderately low heat, tossing, until the spaghetti is thoroughly coated, 3 to 5 minutes; season with salt and pepper. Transfer to shallow bowls and serve right away, passing additional Parmigiano at the table.

This pasta is a lighter take on lasagna. Instead of layering the ingredients, then baking in the oven, Smillie tosses them in a goat cheese sauce, sprinkles Parmigiano-Reggiano on top and crisps the dish briefly under the broiler.

PASTA WITH SHIITAKE, PEAS & GOAT CHEESE

TOTAL *45 min* **MAKES** *6 servings*

1 pound dried lasagnette or broken lasagna noodles

3 tablespoons plus 2 teaspoons extra-virgin olive oil

1 cup peas, thawed if frozen

½ pound thin asparagus, cut into 1-inch pieces

2 tablespoons unsalted butter, plus more for greasing

¾ pound shiitake mushrooms, stems discarded and caps sliced

Kosher salt and freshly ground pepper

2 large shallots, minced (¾ cup)

½ teaspoon finely chopped thyme

2 tablespoons dry white wine

1 tablespoon fresh lemon juice

4 ounces fresh goat cheese

½ cup chopped mint

½ cup freshly grated Parmigiano-Reggiano cheese

PAIR WITH *Minerally Italian white: 2011 Palazzone Orvieto*

1 In a large pot of salted boiling water, cook the lasagnette until al dente. Drain the pasta, reserving 1 cup of the cooking water. Transfer the pasta to a baking sheet and toss with 2 teaspoons of the olive oil.

2 In a medium saucepan of salted boiling water, blanch the peas until crisp-tender, about 3 minutes. Using a slotted spoon, transfer the peas to a plate to cool. Add the asparagus to the saucepan and blanch until they are crisp-tender, about 2 minutes. Drain the asparagus and add them to the peas.

3 Preheat the broiler and butter a shallow 9-by-13-inch baking dish. In a large, deep skillet, heat the remaining 3 tablespoons of olive oil until shimmering. Add the mushrooms, season with salt and pepper and cook over high heat, stirring occasionally, until browned, about 5 minutes. Add the shallots, thyme and the 2 tablespoons of butter and cook, stirring,

until the butter is melted and the shallots are softened, about 3 minutes. Stir in the wine and lemon juice. Remove from the heat; stir in the goat cheese until melted.

4 Fold the asparagus, peas, mint and ¼ cup of the Parmigiano into the sauce and season with salt and pepper. Add the pasta and the reserved cooking water and toss until thoroughly coated. Transfer the pasta to the prepared baking dish and sprinkle the remaining ¼ cup of Parmigiano on top. Broil the lasagnette 6 inches from the heat until lightly golden and bubbling, 3 to 5 minutes. Let rest for 5 minutes before serving.

Smillie makes his Trapanese sauce (a tomato-nut pesto) with mint and buttery, fried Spanish marcona almonds. "I'm a sucker for marconas," he says. He loves the toasty flavor they lend to the pasta sauce.

PASTA WITH SALSA TRAPANESE

TOTAL *45 min* **MAKES** *6 servings*

1 pound tomatoes, cored
2 tablespoons extra-virgin olive oil, plus more for brushing
1 cup marcona almonds
3 tablespoons capers, rinsed and drained
2 garlic cloves, chopped
2 dried red chiles, seeded and chopped
Kosher salt and freshly ground pepper
1 pound penne rigate or bucatini
¼ cup finely chopped mint
¼ cup freshly grated Pecorino Romano cheese, plus more for serving

PAIR WITH *Lively, medium-bodied Italian red: 2010 Castello di Luzzano Carlino Oltrepò Pavese Bonarda*

1 Light a grill or preheat a grill pan. Brush the tomatoes with olive oil and grill over high heat, turning occasionally, until charred all over, 8 to 10 minutes. Transfer the tomatoes to a plate and let cool completely, then coarsely chop them.

2 In a medium skillet, toast the almonds over moderate heat, tossing, until golden, about 5 minutes. Transfer the nuts to a food processor and let cool completely. Add the capers, garlic and chiles and pulse until coarsely chopped. Add the tomatoes and the 2 tablespoons of olive oil and pulse to form a coarse puree; season the tomato pesto with salt and pepper.

3 In a large saucepan of salted boiling water, cook the pasta until al dente. Drain the pasta, reserving ½ cup of the cooking water.

4 In a large bowl, toss the pasta with the tomato pesto, mint, the ¼ cup of grated cheese and the reserved cooking water; season with salt and pepper. Transfer the pasta to bowls and serve, passing additional cheese at the table.

MAKE AHEAD *The tomato pesto can be refrigerated for up to 4 hours. Bring to room temperature before proceeding.*

Smillie is known for the spectacular fresh pastas he makes at Il Buco Alimentari e Vineria, such as the pappardelle here. The chewy texture and wide ribbon shape of pappardelle make it an ideal match for hearty sauces like his chicken thigh ragù on the following page.

FRESH PAPPARDELLE

ACTIVE *40 min*   **TOTAL** *1 hr 30 min*   **MAKES** *¾ pound of pasta*

1½ cups 00 flour, sifted (see Note)
½   teaspoon salt
3   large egg yolks plus 2 large eggs
Semolina flour, for dusting

1 In a food processor, pulse the 00 flour with the salt. In a medium bowl, whisk the egg yolks with the whole eggs and 2 tablespoons of water. Add the eggs to the flour and pulse until the dough just comes together. Transfer the dough to a lightly floured work surface and knead until smooth, about 5 minutes. Cover with plastic wrap and let stand at room temperature for 20 to 30 minutes.

2 Divide the dough into 3 pieces and work with 1 piece at a time, keeping the rest covered. Press the dough to flatten it slightly. Using a pasta machine set at the widest setting, run the dough through successively narrower settings until you reach the thinnest one. Cut the pasta sheet into 10-inch lengths, lay them on a lightly floured work surface and generously dust with semolina. Repeat with the remaining dough.

3 Fold the pasta sheets in half lengthwise, then, using a very sharp knife, cut them into scant ¾-inch-wide ribbons. Transfer the pappardelle to a large baking sheet and dust with more semolina. Let the pappardelle stand at room temperature for 30 minutes before cooking in salted boiling water until al dente, 2 to 3 minutes.

NOTE Doppio zero ("double zero," or 00) flour is a fine Italian flour available at specialty food shops and amazon.com.

Most ragùs require beef, pork or veal—meats that would overwhelm Smillie's light tomato-and-olive sauce here—so he opts for guinea hen or rabbit. Chicken thighs are also tasty and easier to find.

CHICKEN THIGH RAGÙ WITH PAPPARDELLE

ACTIVE *1 hr 45 min* **TOTAL** *3 hr* **MAKES** *6 servings*

½ ounce dried porcini mushrooms
1 tablespoon sugar
2 red onions, chopped
1 fennel bulb—halved, cored and chopped
1 celery rib, chopped
1 carrot, chopped
2 garlic cloves, chopped
1 tablespoon extra-virgin olive oil
½ pound pancetta, cut into ¼-inch dice
2 pounds skinless bone-in chicken thighs, fat trimmed
Kosher salt and freshly ground pepper
1 tablespoon finely chopped rosemary
1 tablespoon finely chopped sage
1 tablespoon tomato paste
¼ cup sherry vinegar
¾ cup dry white wine
2 cups chicken stock or low-sodium broth
1 cup tomato sauce
½ cup pitted Taggiasca or kalamata olives, halved
¾ pound fresh pappardelle (page 194) or dried
Freshly grated Parmigiano-Reggiano cheese, for serving

PAIR WITH *Ripe, juicy Italian white: 2011 Farnese Trebbiano d'Abruzzo*

1 In a small bowl, combine the porcini mushrooms with the sugar, cover with hot water and let soak until the mushrooms have softened, about 30 minutes. Drain and chop the porcini.

2 Meanwhile, in a food processor, combine the onions, fennel, celery, carrot and garlic and pulse until very finely chopped.

3 In a large enameled cast-iron casserole, heat the oil. Add the pancetta and cook over moderate heat, stirring, until browned, about 5 minutes. Using a slotted spoon, transfer the pancetta to a plate.

4 Season the chicken with salt and pepper and add it to the casserole. Cook over moderately high heat, turning once, until golden brown, about 10 minutes. Transfer the chicken to a platter.

5 Pour off all but 2 tablespoons of fat from the casserole. Add the chopped vegetables and a generous pinch each of salt and pepper; cook over moderately low heat until the vegetables are softened and just starting to brown, about 15 minutes. Stir in the rosemary, sage, tomato paste and porcini. Add the vinegar and cook over moderate heat until almost evaporated, about 3 minutes. Add the wine and cook, stirring, until reduced by half, about 3 minutes. Add the stock and tomato sauce and bring to a boil.

6 Return the chicken thighs to the casserole. Cover partially and simmer over low heat until the chicken is very tender, about 1 hour. Transfer the chicken to a platter and let cool slightly, then remove the meat from the bones. Shred the chicken and stir it into the sauce along with the olives and reserved pancetta. Season the ragù with salt and pepper and keep warm.

7 In a large pot of salted boiling water, cook the pappardelle until al dente. Drain well. In a large bowl, gently toss the pappardelle with the ragù and serve, passing freshly grated cheese at the table.

MAKE AHEAD *The ragù can be refrigerated for up to 3 days. Reheat gently before serving.*

This spicy citrus marinade keeps the quail meat juicy while giving it a beautiful char on the grill. The quails are extremely succulent and flavorful and make an elegant first course.

GRILLED SPICED QUAIL WITH SHAVED FENNEL & YOGURT

TOTAL *20 min plus 3 hr marinating*   **MAKES** *4 first-course servings*

½ cup extra-virgin olive oil
½ cup lightly packed parsley leaves
¼ cup fresh orange juice
8 kaffir lime leaves
2 tablespoons oregano leaves
2 garlic cloves
1 tablespoon coriander seeds, crushed
1 tablespoon fennel seeds, crushed
3 fresh or jarred Calabrian chiles (see Note)
Kosher salt and freshly ground pepper
4 semiboneless quail (see Note)
Saba (see Note) or aged balsamic vinegar, for drizzling
Shaved fresh fennel, plain Greek yogurt and lime wedges, for serving

---

PAIR WITH *Bright, cool-climate Pinot Noir: 2011 Tramin*

1 In a blender, combine the olive oil with the parsley, orange juice, kaffir lime leaves, oregano, garlic, coriander seeds, fennel seeds and chiles; puree until nearly smooth, then season with salt and pepper. Transfer the marinade to a large resealable plastic bag, add the quail and turn to coat. Refrigerate for at least 3 hours and up to 8 hours.

2 Light a grill or preheat a grill pan. Remove the quail from the marinade and season with salt and pepper. Grill the quail over high heat, turning once, until the outside is nicely charred and the breast meat is pink, about 5 minutes. Transfer the quail to plates, breast side up. Drizzle a little vinegar over the quail and serve with shaved fennel, yogurt and lime wedges.

NOTE *Spicy red Calabrian chiles and saba, a sweet grape-must reduction, are available at Italian groceries and gourmet food markets. Semiboneless quail usually have had their breast- and backbones removed, but their wing and leg bones are left intact.*

To accompany black bass fillets, Smillie makes this versatile sweet-and-sour relish. You can stuff it in whole fish or pair it with pork, chicken or other firm, white fish fillets.

PAN-ROASTED BLACK BASS WITH CIPOLLINI, FENNEL & RAISIN RELISH

ACTIVE *25 min*   **TOTAL** *50 min*   **MAKES** *4 servings*

½ cup green or golden raisins (see Note)
¼ cup extra-virgin olive oil
2 fennel bulbs—halved, cored and cut into ½-inch dice
4 cipollini onions, peeled and quartered
1 garlic clove, minced
Kosher salt and freshly ground pepper
½ teaspoon finely chopped oregano
1 tablespoon white balsamic vinegar
2 tablespoons finely chopped mint
Four 6-ounce black bass fillets

PAIR WITH *Crisp, citrusy white: 2011 Tasca d'Almerita Regaleali Bianco*

1 In a small bowl, cover the raisins with water and let stand until plumped, about 30 minutes. Drain the raisins, reserving 2 tablespoons of the soaking liquid.

2 Meanwhile, in a medium saucepan, heat 2 tablespoons of the olive oil until shimmering. Add the fennel, onions, garlic and a generous pinch each of salt and pepper. Cook over moderately low heat, stirring occasionally, until the vegetables are very tender, about 20 minutes. Add the raisins and oregano and cook for 30 seconds. Add the white balsamic vinegar and cook until evaporated, about 2 minutes. Stir in the mint and the reserved raisin soaking liquid and season the relish with salt and pepper.

3 In a large nonstick skillet, heat the remaining 2 tablespoons of olive oil until shimmering. Pat the fish dry and season with salt and pepper. Add the fillets to the skillet, skin side down, and cook over high heat for 30 seconds, pressing the fish flat with a spatula. Reduce the heat to moderate and cook until the skin is well browned, about 5 minutes. Turn and cook until the fish is just white throughout, about 3 minutes longer. Transfer the fish to plates, skin side up, top with the relish and serve.

NOTE *Green raisins, also called kishmish, come from Iran, Afghanistan or Pakistan. They are available at some Middle Eastern groceries and khanapakana.com.*

MAKE AHEAD *The cipollini, fennel and raisin relish can be refrigerated for up to 3 days. Bring to room temperature before serving.*

MICHAEL SOLOMONOV

CHEF / OWNER • ZAHAV • PHILADELPHIA

nine years ago, chef Michael Solomonov was cooking Italian food in Philadelphia when he received tragic news: His brother David had been fatally shot while serving in the Israeli army. Until then, Solomonov, who was born near Tel Aviv and raised near Pittsburgh, had never been very interested in the food of his homeland. In the months that followed, however, he felt drawn to the cuisine of his heritage, and even returned to Israel to cook a meal for his brother's fellow soldiers.

Building on the experience, Solomonov came up with the idea for a new restaurant—and an entirely new cooking style. At Zahav, in Philadelphia's Society Hill district, he shares his modern take on Israeli food. It's an approach that includes classic dishes like hummus and kebabs as well as incredibly original ones, like a sweetbread schnitzel with carob and tahini. He uses traditional Israeli techniques—for instance, baking flatbreads in a wood-fired *taboon*—and untraditional touches, such as pickling green tomatoes to add to his tabbouleh (page 208). "We can only be so authentic," says Solomonov. "We're in a completely different hemisphere from Israel, with three fewer growing seasons, forcing us to be creative and whimsical. It's what gives Zahav its identity."

Israelis eat hummus at almost every meal, and Solomonov's versions are incredible. He offers four types at Zahav: sesame seed, fava bean, a buttery Turkish style with grilled garlic and a warm chickpea one enriched with the sesame-seed paste tahini (page 206). Incorporating tahini into hummus is very Israeli, so the dish "becomes more about the earthiness of the chickpeas and sesame seeds, and less about garlic and lemon," Solomonov explains.

Though Zahav is not certified kosher, Solomonov follows some kosher edicts, such as the one against mixing milk and meat in any single dish, which compels him to be more innovative with his recipes. For instance, he wanted his chopped chicken liver to be as smooth and luscious as a pâté, but couldn't use butter or cream for richness as the French do. His solution was to combine schmaltz (the Yiddish term for rendered chicken fat) and chef-y rigor: He purees chicken livers with the schmaltz in a food processor, passes the mixture through a fine-mesh sieve, then cooks it in a warm-water bath in a low oven. He calls the result Schmaltzy Pâté (page 216).

While most of Zahav's menu is Middle Eastern in origin, Solomonov takes ideas from throughout the Jewish diaspora. The pumpkin soup with *fideos* (thin noodles) is Sephardic (Spanish-Jewish) in inspiration—and also vegetarian. He cooks the pumpkin with cloves, cinnamon and ginger, which gives the soup "an implied meatiness—almost like a faux veal stock," he says. The *fideos* thicken the broth, making it even more substantial (page 212).

After the success of Zahav, Solomonov has expanded in Philadelphia with Federal Donuts and Percy Street Barbecue, and he's got plans for an eastern European Jewish restaurant that will actually be kosher. But the food that he serves at Zahav will always be his favorite, he says, because it's the most personal to him. "To be a really good chef you have to live through your food, and it has to have some sort of meaning for you. Michael is taking his life and making it into a cuisine," says Philadelphia chef and empire builder Marc Vetri, Solomonov's mentor. "He makes food that nobody else makes. He's copied no one."

> **To be a really good chef your food has to have some sort of meaning for you. Michael is taking his life and making it into a cuisine that nobody else makes. He's copied no one.**

Solomonov makes his signature hummus at Zahav with an unusually generous amount of tahini—something that distinguishes the hummus of his native Israel from that of other Middle Eastern countries. He tops the dish with warm chickpeas fried with jalapeño, cumin and crushed Aleppo pepper.

HUMMUS WITH TAHINI & SPICY CHICKPEAS

TOTAL *45 min*   **MAKES** *6 servings*

CHICKPEAS

¼ cup extra-virgin olive oil
¼ cup minced Spanish onion
4 garlic cloves, thinly sliced
1 jalapeño—halved lengthwise, seeded and thinly sliced crosswise
One 14-ounce can chickpeas, rinsed and drained
2 tablespoons Aleppo pepper (see Note)
1 teaspoon ground cumin
½ teaspoon ground caraway
½ teaspoon ground coriander
Kosher salt

HUMMUS

¼ cup fresh lemon juice
4 garlic cloves
Two 14-ounce cans chickpeas, rinsed and drained
½ cup tahini
1 tablespoon ground cumin
Kosher salt
2 tablespoons chopped parsley
Lemon wedges and warm pita bread, for serving

1 **PREPARE THE CHICKPEAS** In a medium skillet, heat the olive oil until shimmering. Add the onion, garlic and jalapeño and cook over moderate heat, stirring occasionally, until the vegetables are softened and golden, about 8 minutes. Add the chickpeas, Aleppo pepper, cumin, caraway and coriander and cook, stirring occasionally, until the spices are fragrant and the chickpeas are heated through, about 10 minutes. Season with salt.

2 **MEANWHILE, MAKE THE HUMMUS** In a food processor, combine the lemon juice and garlic and pulse until the garlic is very finely chopped. Let stand for 10 minutes, then add the chickpeas, tahini, cumin and ½ cup of water and puree until smooth. Season with salt.

3 Spoon the hummus onto plates and top with the spicy chickpeas. Garnish with the parsley and serve with lemon wedges and pita bread.

NOTE *Aleppo pepper is a moderately hot crushed dried chile from Syria and Turkey. It is available at gourmet markets and penzeys.com.*

MAKE AHEAD *The hummus and spicy chickpeas can be refrigerated separately overnight. Bring the hummus to room temperature and gently reheat the chickpeas before serving.*

For his twist on the Middle Eastern salad called tabbouleh, Solomonov pickles crunchy green tomatoes instead of using the usual fresh red ones. Also atypical are the walnuts, which add extra crunch and an appealing toasty flavor.

PICKLED GREEN TOMATO, WATERCRESS & WALNUT TABBOULEH

ACTIVE *30 min*   **TOTAL** *1 hr plus overnight pickling*   **MAKES** *6 servings*

TOMATOES

½   cup distilled white vinegar

1   tablespoon honey

1   tablespoon yellow mustard seeds

1   tablespoon kosher salt

4   green tomatoes (2 pounds), sliced crosswise ¼ inch thick

TABBOULEH

1   cup coarse bulgur (5 ounces)

1   cup walnuts (3 ounces)

3   ounces watercress, minced (1 cup)

½   cup minced parsley

½   cup minced dill

½   cup finely chopped red onion

¼   cup extra-virgin olive oil

3   tablespoons fresh lemon juice

Kosher salt

1 **MAKE THE PICKLED TOMATOES** In a medium saucepan, combine the vinegar, honey, mustard seeds, salt and 1 cup of water and bring to a simmer over moderate heat. In a medium heatproof bowl, cover the tomato slices with the hot brine. Let cool completely, then cover and refrigerate the tomatoes overnight.

2 **MAKE THE TABBOULEH** In a medium bowl, cover the bulgur with 2 cups of water and let stand until the grains are plumped and tender, about 1 hour; drain the bulgur well.

3 Meanwhile, in a medium skillet, toast the walnuts over moderate heat, stirring, until golden, about 5 minutes. Let cool, then finely chop the nuts.

4 Drain the green tomatoes and cut them into ¼-inch dice. In a large bowl, toss the bulgur with the pickled tomatoes, chopped walnuts and all of the remaining ingredients. Season the tabbouleh with salt and serve.

MAKE AHEAD *The tabbouleh can be kept at room temperature for up to 4 hours or refrigerated overnight.*

Solomonov marinates smoky, grilled tomatoes in olive oil with mint and red onions. The result is a fabulous make-ahead dish that can be prepared year-round with firm tomatoes. It's wonderful with the crumbled feta over a bed of greens, alongside steak or simply with crusty bread.

GRILLED & MARINATED TOMATOES WITH FETA

TOTAL *30 min plus overnight marinating*   **MAKES** *8 to 10 servings*

4 large, firm tomatoes (2 pounds), sliced crosswise ½ inch thick
1 cup extra-virgin olive oil, plus more for brushing
Kosher salt and freshly ground pepper
¾ cup thinly sliced red onion
¼ cup lightly packed mint leaves
¼ cup distilled white vinegar
¼ cup sugar
1 tablespoon anchovy paste
¼ teaspoon ground allspice
¼ cup chopped parsley
6 ounces feta cheese, preferably Bulgarian, crumbled
Crusty sourdough bread, for serving

PAIR WITH *Vibrant, fruity Spanish rosé: 2011 Muga*

1 Light a grill or preheat a grill pan. Brush the tomato slices with olive oil and season with salt and pepper. Grill over high heat, turning once, until the tomatoes are lightly charred but still firm, about 4 minutes. Transfer to a platter and let cool completely. In a 9-by-13-inch baking dish, layer the tomatoes with the red onion and mint, overlapping the slices slightly.

2 In a small saucepan, whisk the 1 cup of olive oil with the vinegar, sugar, anchovy paste and allspice over moderate heat until the sugar and anchovy dissolve, about 3 minutes. Let the marinade cool completely, then stir in the parsley. Pour the marinade over the tomatoes, cover and refrigerate overnight.

3 Using a slotted spoon or spatula, transfer the tomatoes to a platter or plates. Scatter the feta over the top. Drizzle some of the marinade over the tomatoes and serve with crusty bread.

MAKE AHEAD *The grilled tomatoes can be refrigerated in the marinade for up to 2 days.*

This soup is based on a Sephardic (Spanish-Jewish) recipe Though the dish is vegetarian, cooking the pumpkin with cinnamon and cloves gives the broth an "implied meatiness," says Solomonov. Toasted fideos *(noodles) help thicken the soup and make it even more substantial.*

PUMPKIN SOUP WITH FIDEOS

ACTIVE *45 min*   **TOTAL** *1 hr 30 min*   **MAKES** *6 servings*

¼   cup extra-virgin olive oil
1   Spanish onion, halved lengthwise
     and thinly sliced crosswise
1   celery rib, thinly sliced
4   garlic cloves, thinly sliced
1   tablespoon minced fresh ginger
Kosher salt
1¼   pounds pumpkin or butternut
     squash—peeled, seeded and cut
     into ½-inch dice
2   tablespoons tomato paste
1   tablespoon Urfa or Aleppo pepper
     (see Note)
One 1-inch cinnamon stick
Pinch of ground cloves
8   cups vegetable stock or
     low-sodium broth
4   ounces fideos or capellini,
     broken into 1-inch pieces
½   cup chopped cilantro

1 In a large saucepan, heat the olive oil. Add the onion, celery, garlic, ginger and a generous pinch of salt and cook over moderate heat, stirring occasionally, until the vegetables are softened and well browned, about 15 minutes. Add the pumpkin, tomato paste, Urfa pepper, cinnamon stick and cloves and cook, stirring, until the pumpkin just starts to soften, about 7 minutes. Add the vegetable stock and bring to a boil. Cover and simmer over moderately low heat for about 40 minutes, stirring occasionally. Discard the cinnamon stick.

2 Meanwhile, preheat the oven to 325°. Spread the *fideos* on a rimmed baking sheet and bake for about 10 minutes, until well browned and nutty-smelling.

3 Add the toasted *fideos* to the soup and cook over moderate heat until the noodles are al dente, 7 to 10 minutes. Stir in the cilantro and season with salt. Ladle the soup into bowls and serve.

NOTE *Urfa and Aleppo peppers are crushed dried chiles from Turkey and Syria, respectively; Urfa is slightly hotter than Aleppo. Both are available at gourmet markets and* amazon.com.

MAKE AHEAD *The soup can be refrigerated overnight. Reheat gently before serving.*

These spicy, tangy cooked carrots are fragrant with cumin, caraway and mint. At Zahav, Solomonov offers them as meze (small plates), but he also recommends serving them tossed with greens as a salad, or alongside chicken or salmon in charmoula (page 220).

MOROCCAN CARROTS

ACTIVE *20 min* **TOTAL** *1 hr 45 min* **MAKES** *4 servings*

2 tablespoons grapeseed oil
2 garlic cloves, minced
1 tablespoon ground cumin
1 teaspoon ground caraway
5 large carrots (1½ pounds), halved crosswise
Kosher salt
½ teaspoon finely grated orange zest plus 2 tablespoons orange juice
½ teaspoon finely grated lemon zest plus 2 tablespoons lemon juice
1 jalapeño—halved lengthwise, seeded and thinly sliced crosswise
2 tablespoons finely chopped cilantro
2 tablespoons finely chopped mint

1 In a large, deep skillet, heat the oil. Add the garlic, cumin and caraway and cook over moderately low heat until fragrant, 1 minute. Add the carrots, a generous pinch of salt and enough water to just cover the carrots and bring to a boil. Simmer over moderately low heat, turning once, until crisp-tender, 12 to 15 minutes. Using tongs, transfer the carrots to a plate. Let cool completely, then cut into ½-inch rounds.

2 Meanwhile, boil the braising liquid over moderately high heat until reduced to ½ cup, about 15 minutes. Stir in the orange and lemon zest and juice.

3 In a serving bowl, toss the carrots with the jalapeño and the reduced braising liquid and season with salt. Refrigerate until well chilled, about 1 hour. Stir in the cilantro and mint and serve.

MAKE AHEAD *The carrots can be refrigerated overnight. Add the herbs just before serving.*

Solomonov follows some kosher guidelines at Zahav and doesn't mix dairy with meat. To make his chopped chicken liver as luxurious as pâté, he adds schmaltz (rendered chicken fat) to chicken livers for richness instead of butter or cream, then passes the result through a sieve to make it ultrasmooth.

SCHMALTZY PÂTÉ

TOTAL *1 hr plus 6 hr chilling*   **MAKES** *8 servings as an hors d'oeuvre*

¼ cup fresh lemon juice

2 tablespoons honey

Kosher salt

1 tablespoon finely chopped dill

1 large carrot, halved lengthwise and thinly sliced crosswise

¼ cup rendered chicken fat (schmaltz; see Note)

1 Spanish onion, halved and thinly sliced

½ pound chicken livers—trimmed, rinsed and patted dry

2 large eggs

½ pound sliced challah bread, toasted and cut into 2-inch strips

PAIR WITH *Strawberry-scented* cru *Beaujolais: 2010 Villa Ponciago Fleurie*

1 In a small saucepan, combine the lemon juice, honey, 1 tablespoon of salt and ½ cup of water and bring to a boil. Stir in the dill. In a heatproof bowl, pour the brine over the sliced carrot and let stand for at least 6 hours or refrigerate overnight.

2 Meanwhile, preheat the oven to 325°. In a medium skillet, melt the schmaltz. Add the onion and a generous pinch of salt and cook over moderate heat, stirring occasionally, until softened and well browned, about 13 minutes. Scrape the onion and schmaltz into a food processor and let cool completely. Add the chicken livers, eggs and 1 teaspoon of salt and puree until smooth. Pass the puree through a fine sieve into a bowl.

3 Line a 6-by-3-inch porcelain terrine or a 5-inch ceramic ramekin with plastic wrap and set it in an 8-inch square baking dish. Pour the chicken liver puree into the lined terrine. Transfer the baking dish to the oven and carefully pour

in enough hot water to reach halfway up the sides of the terrine. Bake for 35 to 40 minutes, until the pâté is browned on top and set. Remove the terrine from the baking dish and refrigerate until the pâté is well chilled, at least 6 hours.

4 Drain the pickled carrot. Turn the pâté out onto a plate and peel off the plastic wrap. Serve with challah toasts and the pickled carrot.

NOTE *Schmaltz is available in the refrigerated section of most supermarkets.*

MAKE AHEAD *The pickled carrot and pâté can be refrigerated separately for up to 2 days.*

Solomonov flavors the warm potato-and-egg salad here with a red wine vinaigrette, then spices it with za'atar, a Middle Eastern blend of sesame seeds, herbs and sumac.

GRILLED BRANZINO FILLETS WITH POTATO & SPINACH SALAD

ACTIVE *30 min* **TOTAL** *1 hr* **MAKES** *4 servings*

3 large Yukon Gold potatoes
Kosher salt
1 large egg
1 cup packed baby spinach
2 celery ribs, thinly sliced
2 tablespoons minced red onion
2½ tablespoons red wine vinegar
2 teaspoons za'atar (see Note)
⅓ cup extra-virgin olive oil, plus
  more for brushing
½ teaspoon Aleppo pepper
  (see Note on page 212)
¼ teaspoon ground fenugreek
Four 4-ounce branzino fillets with skin

PAIR WITH *Citrusy, minerally Sancerre: 2011 Alphonse Mellot La Moussière Blanc*

1 In a medium saucepan, cover the potatoes with water, add a large pinch of salt and bring to a boil. Cook over moderate heat until tender, 25 to 30 minutes. Drain the potatoes and let cool slightly, then peel and cut them into ½-inch dice.

2 Meanwhile, in a small saucepan, cover the egg with water and bring to a boil. Simmer over moderate heat for 10 minutes. Drain and cool under running water, then peel and coarsely chop the egg.

3 In a medium bowl, toss the potatoes with the egg, spinach, celery, onion, vinegar, za'atar and the ⅓ cup of olive oil. Season the potato salad with salt.

4 Light a grill or preheat a grill pan. In a small bowl, combine the Aleppo pepper and fenugreek. Brush the fish with olive oil, sprinkle on both sides with the spice mixture and season with salt. Grill the fish skin side down over high heat until the skin is crisp, 3 to 4 minutes. Turn the fish and cook just until white throughout, about 1 minute longer. Transfer the branzino to plates and serve with the potato and spinach salad.

NOTE *Za'atar is a Middle Eastern blend of sesame seeds, herbs and sumac. It is available at Middle Eastern markets and penzeys.com.*

Treating Israeli couscous like risotto, Solomonov simmers the pearl-shaped grains in a tomato sauce until they become rich and creamy. The side is incredibly tasty with the salmon marinated in charmoula, a tangy, cilantro-based Moroccan sauce.

SALMON IN CHARMOULA WITH RISOTTO-STYLE ISRAELI COUSCOUS

TOTAL *1 hr plus overnight marinating* **MAKES** *4 servings*

SALMON

- ¼ cup chopped cilantro
- ¼ cup canola oil
- 2 garlic cloves
- 1 tablespoon minced fresh ginger
- 1½ teaspoons sweet paprika
- 1 teaspoon kosher salt
- ½ teaspoon turmeric
- ½ teaspoon ground cumin
- Four 5-ounce skinless salmon fillets

TAHINI SAUCE

- 1 tablespoon extra-virgin olive oil
- ¼ cup thinly sliced cremini mushrooms
- 2 garlic cloves, thinly sliced
- 1 tablespoon tahini
- 1 tablespoon fresh lemon juice
- 1 tablespoon finely chopped dill
- Kosher salt

COUSCOUS

- 1 cup Israeli couscous (6 ounces)
- ¼ cup extra-virgin olive oil
- ½ cup finely chopped Spanish onion
- Pinch of cinnamon
- Kosher salt
- ½ cup tomato puree
- 1½ cups warm water

PAIR WITH *Peach-scented, full-bodied French white: 2010 Domaine de Triennes Sainte Fleur Viognier*

1 PREPARE THE SALMON In a blender, combine the cilantro, canola oil, garlic, ginger, paprika, salt, turmeric and cumin and puree until smooth. Pour the marinade into a resealable plastic bag, add the salmon and seal the bag. Turn to coat the fish and refrigerate overnight.

2 MAKE THE TAHINI SAUCE In a small skillet, heat the olive oil. Add the mushrooms and garlic and cook over moderately low heat, stirring, until the mushrooms are well browned, about 10 minutes. Scrape the mushrooms and garlic into a blender and let cool. Add the tahini, lemon juice and ⅓ cup of water and puree until smooth. Stir in the dill and season the sauce with salt.

3 PREPARE THE COUSCOUS In a medium saucepan, toast the couscous over moderate heat, tossing, until golden, about 10 minutes. Transfer to a small bowl. In the same saucepan, heat the olive oil. Add the onion and a pinch each of cinnamon and salt and cook over moderately low heat, stirring occasionally, until the onion is softened and just starting to brown, about 8 minutes. Add the toasted couscous and cook for 1 minute, stirring, then stir in the tomato puree. Add the water ½ cup at a time and stir constantly over moderately low heat, allowing the liquid to be absorbed between additions, until the couscous is al dente, about 20 minutes. Season with salt and keep warm; add 1 or 2 tablespoons of water if the couscous seems dry.

4 Light a grill or preheat a grill pan. Scrape the marinade off the salmon, season the fish with salt and grill over high heat, turning once, until lightly charred and nearly cooked through, 3 to 5 minutes. Spoon the couscous onto plates, top with the salmon, drizzle with the tahini sauce and serve.

MAKE AHEAD *The tahini sauce can be refrigerated overnight. Bring to room temperature before serving.*

Solomonov braises lamb shanks with sweet date molasses until the meat is tender, then adds tangy rhubarb to the sauce. The dish can also be prepared with tart fruits like quince or crabapples when rhubarb isn't in season.

BRAISED LAMB SHANKS WITH PEAS, MINT & RHUBARB

ACTIVE *30 min* **TOTAL** *4 hr* **MAKES** *4 servings*

¼ cup extra-virgin olive oil

4 lamb shanks (5 pounds total)

½ teaspoon cinnamon

Kosher salt and freshly ground
   black pepper

1 Spanish onion, halved and
   thinly sliced

1 celery rib, sliced ¼ inch thick

4 garlic cloves, thinly sliced

3 tablespoons date molasses
   (see Note) or pure maple syrup

2 medium rhubarb stalks
   (5 ounces), sliced ¾ inch thick

1 cup frozen peas, thawed

¼ cup finely chopped mint

Steamed rice, for serving

PAIR WITH *Berry-scented Syrah blend: 2010 Musar Jeune Red*

1 Preheat the oven to 325°. In a large enameled cast-iron casserole, heat the olive oil until shimmering. Rub each lamb shank with ⅛ teaspoon of the cinnamon and season with salt and pepper. Add the lamb shanks to the casserole and cook over moderately high heat until browned on all sides, about 12 minutes. Transfer to a platter.

2 Add the onion, celery and garlic to the casserole and cook over moderate heat, stirring occasionally, until the vegetables are softened and well browned, about 15 minutes. Stir in the date molasses and 2 cups of water and bring to a boil. Add the lamb and any accumulated juices and cover. Braise in the oven for 3 hours, turning once, until the meat is very tender.

3 Scatter the rhubarb and peas over the lamb in the casserole. Cover and braise for 15 minutes longer, until the rhubarb is tender. Transfer the lamb shanks to plates or a platter. Stir the mint into the vegetables and season with salt and pepper. Spoon the sauce and vegetables over the lamb and serve with steamed rice.

NOTE *Date molasses is a complex, sweet and intensely flavored syrup made from dates. It is available at Middle Eastern markets and kalustyans.com.*

MAKE AHEAD *The recipe can be prepared through Step 2 and refrigerated overnight. Bring to room temperature before proceeding.*

"I like to karate-chop diners with something different at the end of the meal," *Solomonov says. He does that with this cool dessert of rose-scented rhubarb and honeydew melon granita topped with creamy* lebneh *(a soft, yogurt-like fresh cheese) and crunchy candied pistachios.*

POACHED RHUBARB WITH MELON GRANITA

ACTIVE *45 min* **TOTAL** *3 hr 15 min* **MAKES** *6 servings*

1 cup plus 2 tablespoons sugar
¾ pound Galia or honeydew melon—halved, seeded, peeled and cut into 1-inch pieces
Kosher salt
1 vanilla bean, split and seeds scraped
1 teaspoon rose water
1 pound rhubarb, cut into ½-inch dice (see Note)
½ cup shelled unsalted pistachios
⅓ cup lebneh (see Note) or plain whole-milk Greek yogurt
1 tablespoon honey

1 In a medium saucepan, combine 1 cup of the sugar with 1 cup of water and bring to a boil; simmer until the sugar is dissolved, about 3 minutes. In a blender, combine the melon with ¼ cup of the hot syrup and a pinch of salt and puree until smooth. Pour the melon puree into a square metal baking pan and freeze until solid, at least 3 hours.

2 Meanwhile, add the vanilla bean and seeds and the rose water to the remaining syrup in the saucepan and bring to a boil. Simmer over low heat for 10 minutes. Stir in the rhubarb and simmer over moderately low heat, stirring occasionally, until the rhubarb is just softened, about 7 minutes. Remove from the heat and let cool completely. Discard the vanilla bean. Refrigerate the rhubarb in the syrup until well chilled, about 1 hour.

3 In a medium saucepan, combine the remaining 2 tablespoons of sugar with 1 tablespoon of water and bring to a boil. When the sugar is dissolved, stir in the pistachios and cook over moderate heat, stirring occasionally to break up the clumps, until the nuts are glazed in a deep amber caramel, about 7 minutes. Transfer the candied pistachios to a plate and season with salt. Let cool completely, then break up any clumps.

4 Remove the granita from the freezer and let stand at room temperature until it just starts to soften, about 10 minutes. Using a fork, scrape the granita into icy flakes.

5 In a medium bowl, whisk the *lebneh* with the honey. To serve, spoon the chilled rhubarb and its syrup into glasses and top with the *lebneh*, granita and candied pistachios.

NOTE *If fresh rhubarb isn't available, frozen can be used. Lebneh is a yogurt-like fresh Lebanese cheese. It is available at specialty and health food stores.*

MAKE AHEAD *The granita can be frozen for up to 1 week. The poached rhubarb can be refrigerated in its syrup for up to 3 days. The candied pistachios can be stored in an airtight container at room temperature for up to 5 days.*

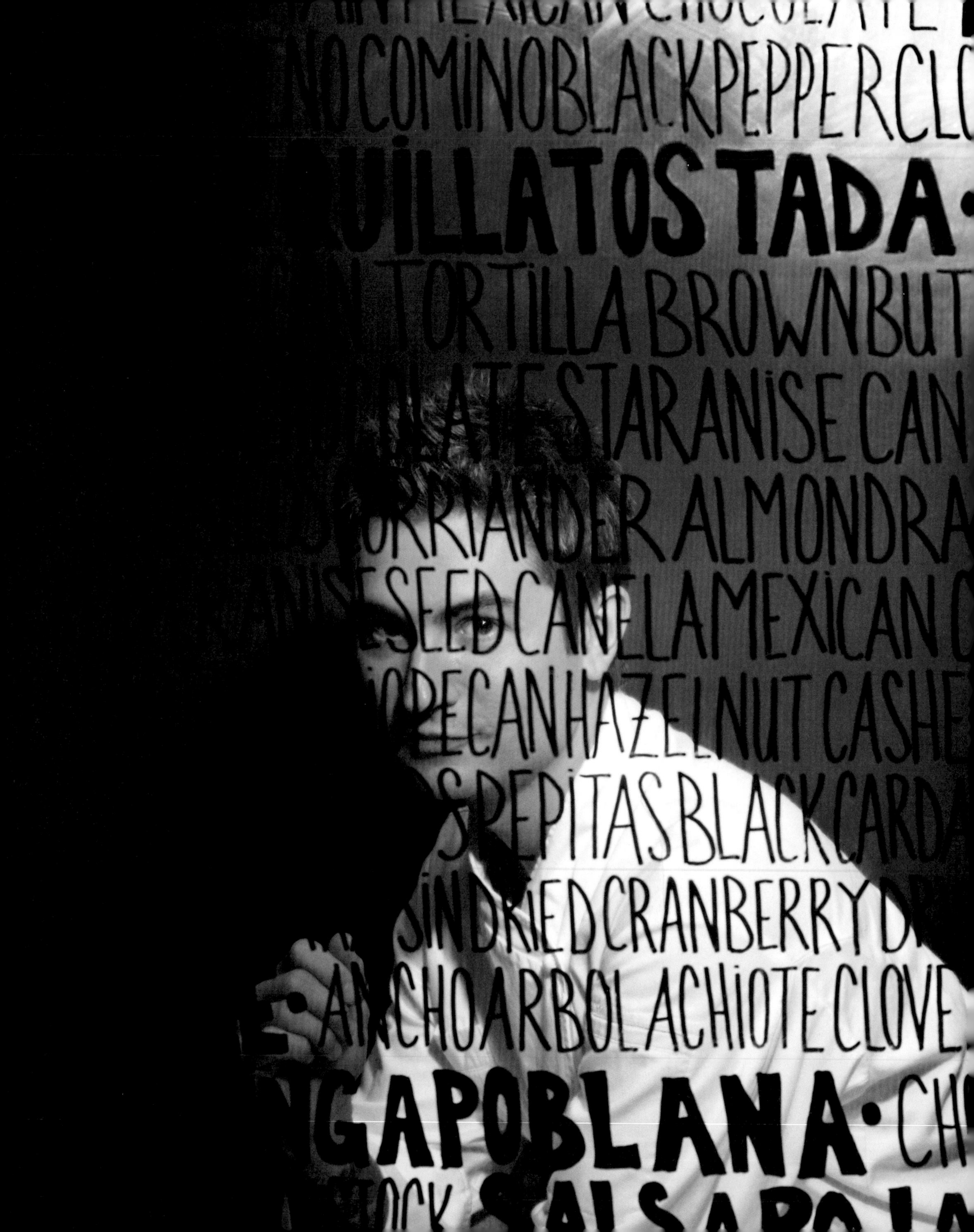
COMINOBLACKPEPPERCL
ILLATOSTADA
TORTILLA BROWNBUT
STARANISE CAN
RRIANDER ALMONDRA
SEED CANELAMEXICAN
ECANHAZELNUT CASHE
SPEPITASBLACKCARD
SINDRIEDCRANBERRY
ANCHOARBOLACHIOTE CLOVE
GAPOBLANA

ALEX STUPAK

CHEF / OWNER • EMPELLÓN COCINA AND EMPELLÓN TAQUERIA • NEW YORK CITY

known for his avant-garde desserts at Chicago's Alinea and New York City's WD-50, Alex Stupak was one of America's most acclaimed pastry chefs. Then, in 2011, he did something unexpected: He left molecular gastronomy behind to open an ambitious taqueria. Stupak, who has no Mexican heritage, is the chef and owner of Manhattan's Empellón Taqueria and its new offshoot, Empellón Cocina, where he smartly expands the boundaries of Mexican cuisine. At Empellón Taqueria, Stupak fills tacos with sweetbreads and chorizo gravy or wild spinach and macadamia nut hummus; at Empellón Cocina, he blends squid ink into his idiosyncratic version of mole and tops cornmeal crackers with shrimp and sea urchin mousse. "Alex is expressing his love of Mexican cuisine in a very personal way," says chef Wylie Dufresne of WD-50. "You can't get his style of food anywhere else because no one else is doing what he's doing."

Stupak has been an intense, overachieving cook from a young age. In high school he worked at Denny's, where he was chewed out for using real eggs to make omelets instead of the processed kind. He simply found himself unable to compromise on food because he felt such an intense personal relationship to it. "Cooking is my method of connecting with people," he explains. "It's the way I communicate." As a student at the Culinary Institute of America in upstate New York, he was drawn to the most technical discipline, pastry, and ended up excelling in the hyper-intellectual field of modernist cooking.

After learning all he could about molecular pastry by the age of 30, Stupak started looking for a new challenge. A vacation in Oaxaca, Mexico, provided inspiration. He took the trip with his wife, Lauren Resler (now Empellón's pastry chef), whose mother is Mexican. He compares the excitement he felt on that visit to his first time working with black truffles: "The thought process behind the dishes was so modern." To an outsider, modernist cuisine and Mexican cooking might seem worlds apart, but Stupak was struck by the similarities. "It's not just about flavor, it's about technique," says Stupak, who has since traveled to Mexico around a dozen times to learn more about traditional cooking methods. "The focus is on transforming ingredients instead of just highlighting their quality."

Despite the complexity of many of Stupak's dishes, his recipes can also reinvent flavors in surprisingly simple ways. For his riff on smoked salmon (page 236), Stupak cures salmon fillet with two smoky ingredients: finely ground chipotle powder and the fire-roasted Mexican spirit mezcal. Every day at his restaurants he serves at least seven different salsas, including one made with smoked cashews, and another, called *sikil pak* (page 230), that's a nutty, spicy blend of pumpkin seeds and roasted tomatoes. Even though he pushes the borders of regional Mexican food, his recipes honor the cuisine's essential character. For his meatballs in *tinga poblana* (page 244), for instance, he roasts tomatoes and garlic until blistered, purees them along with chipotles to make a sauce, then adds chorizo. "Close your eyes," Dufresne says about the best way to taste the dish. "The aromas, flavors and emotions of Mexican food are all still there."

Will Stupak one day tire of cooking Mexican dishes in the way he moved on from pastry? No, he says. "Mexican cuisine is an inexhaustible source of inspiration. I'll never learn everything about it and I'm not even close to accomplishing what I want to with Empellón."

> “ Alex is expressing his love of Mexican cuisine in a very personal way. You can't get his style of food anywhere else in the world because no one else is doing what he's doing.

Stupak prepares this outstanding Yucatán-style dip (called sikil pak in Mayan) by pureeing pumpkin seeds (sikil) with roasted tomatoes (pak), garlic and chile. Typically served with tortilla chips, it also makes a healthy vegan accompaniment for vegetables.

TOASTED PUMPKIN SEED DIP

TOTAL *30 min*　**MAKES** *6 servings*

2　plum tomatoes
2　unpeeled garlic cloves
1　small green habanero chile
½　pound raw pumpkin seeds
　　(1½ cups)
2　tablespoons fresh orange juice
¼　cup minced white onion,
　　rinsed and blotted dry
¼　cup finely chopped cilantro
Pinch of cinnamon
Kosher salt
Tortilla chips, for serving

1 Preheat a small cast-iron skillet or griddle. Add the tomatoes, garlic cloves and habanero and roast over high heat, turning occasionally, until the vegetables are softened and charred in spots, about 12 minutes. Transfer to a plate; let cool.

2 Meanwhile, in a large skillet, toast the pumpkin seeds over moderate heat, tossing, until lightly browned, 5 to 7 minutes. Transfer the pumpkin seeds to a food processor and let cool completely. Pulse the seeds until a coarse puree forms, then transfer to a medium bowl.

3 Halve the habanero and remove the seeds. Peel the garlic and add it to the food processor along with the tomatoes, habanero and orange juice; puree until smooth. Stir the puree into the ground pumpkin seeds along with the onion, cilantro and cinnamon. Transfer the dip to a serving bowl, season with salt and serve with tortilla chips.

MAKE AHEAD *The dip can be refrigerated overnight. Serve at room temperature.*

"My favorite flavor is crunchy," Stupak says. To add that texture to his excellent, otherwise classic guacamole, he stirs in toasted chopped pistachios, which also contribute a delicious nuttiness.

GUACAMOLE WITH PISTACHIOS

TOTAL *20 min*   **MAKES** *4 to 6 servings*

2 tablespoons extra-virgin olive oil
½ cup unsalted shelled pistachios, coarsely chopped
Kosher salt
3 Hass avocados, halved and pitted
¼ cup minced white onion, rinsed and blotted dry
2 jalapeños, seeded and minced
2 tablespoons fresh lime juice
½ cup chopped cilantro, plus more for garnish
Tortilla chips, for serving

1 In a medium skillet, heat the olive oil until shimmering. Add the pistachios and cook, stirring, until lightly toasted, about 3 minutes. Using a slotted spoon, transfer the pistachios to paper towels to drain; reserve the oil in the skillet. Season the pistachios with salt.

2 Scoop the avocados into a medium bowl and coarsely mash with a fork. Stir in the onion, jalapeños, lime juice, ½ cup of cilantro and all but 2 tablespoons of the pistachios; season with salt. Scrape the guacamole into a serving bowl and drizzle some of the reserved oil on top. Garnish with chopped cilantro and the remaining 2 tablespoons of pistachios and serve with tortilla chips.

When he makes this stunning salad at Empellón Cocina, Stupak roasts baby carrots with mole poblano, *a complex sauce that includes dried chiles, raisins and chocolate. Here, the carrots are simply roasted with smoky canned chipotles in adobo, then served with peppery watercress and cooling yogurt.*

CHIPOTLE-ROASTED BABY CARROTS

ACTIVE *20 min* **TOTAL** *1 hr* **MAKES** *6 servings*

30 thin baby carrots (2 to 3 bunches),
      tops discarded, carrots scrubbed
2 chipotle chiles in adobo,
      minced, plus 1 teaspoon of adobo
      sauce from the can
1 tablespoon unsulfured molasses
2½ tablespoons extra-virgin olive oil
Kosher salt and freshly ground
      black pepper
3 tablespoons sesame seeds
4 ounces watercress, thick stems
      discarded
Plain Greek yogurt, for serving

1 Preheat the oven to 350°. Toss the carrots on a rimmed baking sheet with the chipotles, molasses and 2 tablespoons of the olive oil; season with salt and pepper. Roast for 30 to 35 minutes, until the carrots are crisp-tender and browned. Transfer the carrots to a plate and let them cool completely.

2 Meanwhile, in a small skillet, toast the sesame seeds over moderate heat, tossing, until golden, 3 to 5 minutes. Stir in the remaining ½ tablespoon of olive oil and season with salt; let cool.

3 On the plate, toss the carrots with the 1 teaspoon of adobo sauce. Arrange the carrots on 6 plates and scatter the watercress on top. Garnish with the sesame seeds and serve with yogurt.

MAKE AHEAD *The roasted carrots can be kept at room temperature for up to 4 hours.*

Instead of smoking salmon, Stupak ingeniously adds smokiness with chipotles and mezcal (a tequila-like spirit), then serves the silky salmon with a crisp sorrel salad drizzled with a lime and cream cheese dressing. "Either a bagel or a tortilla would be suitable with this dish," he says.

MEZCAL-CURED SALMON WITH SORREL SALAD

TOTAL *30 min plus 9 hr curing*   **MAKES** *8 first-course servings*

SALMON
One 12-ounce skinless salmon fillet
½ cup mezcal
3 dried chipotle chiles—stemmed, seeded and torn into small pieces
¼ cup kosher salt

SALAD
2 ounces cream cheese, at room temperature
2 tablespoons fresh lime juice
Kosher salt
4 ounces small sorrel leaves (see Note)
¼ cup thinly sliced red onion

PAIR WITH *Clean, dry rosé: 2011 Commanderie de Peyrassol*

1 PREPARE THE SALMON Set the salmon fillet in a glass or ceramic baking dish. Brush the fish all over with ¼ cup of the mezcal, then cover with plastic wrap and refrigerate for 1 hour.

2 In a spice grinder, combine the dried chipotles with the kosher salt and grind to a fine powder. Sprinkle both sides of the salmon with the chipotle salt, then cover with plastic wrap and refrigerate for 4 hours longer.

3 Brush the salmon with the remaining ¼ cup of mezcal and tightly wrap the fillet in plastic. Refrigerate for at least 4 hours or overnight.

4 Unwrap the salmon. On a work surface, using a very sharp, thin knife, cut the fish at an angle crosswise into very thin slices. Arrange the slices on a platter.

5 MAKE THE SALAD In a blender or food processor, puree the cream cheese with the lime juice and 2 tablespoons of water. Season with salt. In a bowl, toss the sorrel with the red onion and the dressing. Serve the salad alongside the salmon.

NOTE *If sorrel is unavailable, use baby spinach.*

MAKE AHEAD *The salmon can be prepared through Step 3 and refrigerated for up to 4 days.*

"Seafood with cheese is taboo for many cooks," Stupak says, *"but Mexican cuisine disregards that rule."* So, too, does Stupak by pairing *Jack cheese with plump shrimp for his* queso fundido, *a Mexican rendition of fondue.*

QUESO FUNDIDO WITH SHRIMP & TOMATOES

TOTAL *25 min*   **MAKES** *4 to 6 servings*

2 teaspoons extra-virgin olive oil
1 small onion, halved and thinly sliced
1 garlic clove, minced
1 serrano chile—halved, seeded and thinly sliced
Kosher salt
3 plum tomatoes, diced
1½ tablespoons finely chopped oregano
2 dozen medium shrimp, shelled and deveined
1 pound Monterey Jack cheese, shredded
Warm corn or flour tortillas, for serving

PAIR WITH *Zippy, citrusy sparkling wine: NV German Gilabert Cava*

1 In a large nonstick skillet, heat the oil until shimmering. Add the onion, garlic, chile and a generous pinch of salt and cook over moderate heat until the onion is softened and just lightly browned, about 8 minutes. Add the tomatoes and oregano and cook until the tomatoes just start to break down, about 5 minutes.

2 Season the shrimp with salt. Nestle them in the tomato sauce and cook over moderate heat, turning once, until just curled and opaque throughout, about 4 minutes. Add the cheese and cook over low heat, stirring, until the cheese is melted. Season the *queso fundido* with salt, transfer to bowls and serve at once, with warm tortillas.

In Mexico, cooks serve this quick casserole of fried tortillas and salsa as a brunch dish with eggs. Stupak omits the eggs and instead combines hen-of-the-woods mushrooms with a spicy, rich salsa made from pasilla chiles, resulting in a light but satisfying vegetarian main course.

CHILAQUILES WITH PASILLA SALSA & HEN-OF-THE-WOODS MUSHROOMS

ACTIVE *45 min*   **TOTAL** *1 hr 15 min*   **MAKES** *4 to 6 servings*

4 pasilla chiles, stemmed
    and seeded (see Note)
4 plum tomatoes
4 unpeeled garlic cloves
¼ cup canola oil
Kosher salt and freshly ground pepper
½ pound hen-of-the-woods
    mushrooms (maitake), *separated
    into bite-size pieces*
One 13-ounce bag corn tortilla chips,
    crushed into ½-inch pieces
Crumbled queso fresco, *Mexican
    crema (or sour cream)
    and chopped white onion and
    cilantro, for garnish*

1 Preheat a large cast-iron skillet or griddle. Add the pasillas and toast over high heat, pressing them down with a spatula and turning once, until pliable and fragrant, about 1 minute. Transfer the pasillas to a heatproof bowl and cover with 2 cups of hot water. Let stand for about 30 minutes, until the pasillas are completely rehydrated.

2 Meanwhile, in the same skillet, roast the tomatoes and garlic over high heat until charred, about 12 minutes.

3 Transfer the rehydrated pasillas to a blender and add 1 cup of their soaking liquid. Puree until smooth, then strain through a coarse sieve into a bowl.

4 In a large skillet, heat 1 tablespoon of the oil. Add the pasilla puree and cook over moderate heat, stirring occasionally, until deep red and reduced nearly to a paste, about 15 minutes.

5 Peel the roasted garlic and add it to the blender along with the tomatoes. Puree until smooth, then strain through a coarse sieve into the skillet with the pasilla paste; bring to a boil. Simmer the salsa over moderately low heat for 15 minutes, stirring occasionally. Season with salt and pepper and keep warm.

6 In another large skillet, heat the remaining 3 tablespoons of oil until shimmering. Add the mushrooms, season with salt and pepper and cook, stirring occasionally, until the mushrooms are browned, 3 to 5 minutes. Stir in the pasilla salsa and bring to a simmer. Add the crushed tortilla chips and cook, tossing, for 3 minutes. Transfer the *chilaquiles* to a platter or plates and garnish with *queso fresco, crema* and chopped onion and cilantro. Serve right away.

——
NOTE *Pasillas are long, black dried chiles with a fruity, herbaceous flavor. They are available at Latin markets.*

Stupak calls parsley-flecked green chorizo the "vegetal cousin" of the more commonly seen red variety. Here, he sautés the crumbled sausage with kale and fingerling potatoes for an exceptional taco filling.

HOMEMADE GREEN CHORIZO TACOS WITH KALE & POTATOES

ACTIVE *50 min*   **TOTAL** *1 hr 15 min plus overnight chilling*   **MAKES** *4 to 6 servings*

GREEN CHORIZO

- ⅛ teaspoon black peppercorns
- ⅛ teaspoon coriander seeds
- ⅛ teaspoon dried oregano
- 1 bay leaf, crushed
- 1 clove
- 2 unpeeled garlic cloves
- 1 small poblano chile
- 1 cup lightly packed parsley leaves
- 2 tablespoons sherry vinegar

Kosher salt

- ¾ pound ground pork shoulder

FILLING

- 1 pound fingerling potatoes, sliced crosswise into ½-inch rounds
- ¼ cup extra-virgin olive oil

Kosher salt and freshly ground pepper

- 2 garlic cloves, minced
- ¾ pound kale, stems discarded and leaves chopped
- 12 warm corn tortillas

Crumbled *queso fresco and Mexican crema (or sour cream), for serving*

PAIR WITH *Fresh, berry-rich Malbec: 2009 Catena Zapata*

1 MAKE THE GREEN CHORIZO In a small skillet, toast the peppercorns, coriander seeds, oregano, bay leaf and clove over moderate heat until fragrant, about 2 minutes. Transfer the spices to a spice grinder and let cool completely, then finely grind them.

2 In the same skillet, roast the garlic cloves over high heat, turning, until tender and charred in spots, about 10 minutes. Let the garlic cool, then peel and transfer the cloves to a blender.

3 Roast the poblano directly over a gas flame or under a preheated broiler, turning, until charred all over. Let cool, then peel, stem and seed the chile. Add the chile, parsley, sherry vinegar and 1½ teaspoons of salt to the blender and puree until smooth.

4 In a medium bowl, mix the ground pork with the puree and the spices. Press a piece of plastic wrap directly onto the green chorizo and refrigerate overnight.

5 MAKE THE FILLING Preheat the oven to 350°. On a rimmed baking sheet, toss the potatoes with 1 tablespoon of the olive oil and season with salt and pepper. Roast for about 30 minutes, tossing once, until golden and tender.

6 In a large skillet, heat the remaining 3 tablespoons of olive oil. Add the garlic and the green chorizo and cook over moderately high heat, breaking up the chorizo with a spoon, until it is just starting to brown, about 10 minutes. Add the kale and toss until just wilted, then add ⅓ cup of water. Cook over moderately low heat, stirring occasionally, until the kale is tender and the chorizo is cooked, about 10 minutes. Fold in the potatoes and season with salt and pepper.

7 Spoon the filling onto the tortillas and serve with *queso fresco* and *crema.*

MAKE AHEAD *The uncooked green chorizo can be refrigerated for up to 2 days or frozen for up to 1 month.*

In Mexico's Puebla region, cooks usually prepare tinga *(a zesty, tomatoey stew) with chicken, pork or vegetables. Stupak stirs chorizo into the traditional sauce, then adds* albóndigas *(meatballs) to create a hearty dish that looks Italian but tastes undeniably Mexican.*

OVEN-ROASTED MEATBALLS WITH TINGA POBLANA

ACTIVE *1 hr*   **TOTAL** *1 hr 45 min*   **MAKES** *6 servings*

TINGA

- 2 pounds plum tomatoes (about 4)
- 6 unpeeled garlic cloves
- 3 chipotle chiles in adobo, seeded and minced
- 1 tablespoon extra-virgin olive oil
- 1 small white onion, minced
- ½ pound fresh Mexican-style chorizo, casings removed
- 2 cups chicken stock or low-sodium broth
- 1 bay leaf
- Kosher salt and freshly ground pepper

MEATBALLS

- 1 large egg
- ½ cup milk
- ½ cup finely crushed tortilla chips (1 ounce)
- ¼ cup shredded Cotija or pecorino cheese (1 ounce)
- 4 garlic cloves, minced
- 1 teaspoon dried oregano
- Salt and freshly ground pepper
- ¾ pound ground pork
- ¾ pound ground beef
- Warm corn tortillas, for serving

PAIR WITH *Juicy, full-bodied Spanish red: 2010 Bodegas Juan Gil Monastrell*

1 **MAKE THE TINGA** Preheat a large cast-iron skillet or griddle. Add the tomatoes and garlic cloves and roast over high heat, turning occasionally, until softened and charred in spots, about 12 minutes; let cool slightly. Peel the garlic and transfer it to a blender along with the tomatoes and chipotles; puree until smooth.

2 In a large saucepan, heat the olive oil. Add the onion and cook over moderate heat, stirring, until lightly golden, about 5 minutes. Add the chorizo and cook over moderately high heat, stirring to break up the meat, until no trace of pink remains, about 5 minutes. Stir in the tomato puree, stock and bay leaf and bring to a boil. Simmer over low heat until the sauce is thickened, about 1 hour. Discard the bay leaf and season the *tinga* with salt and pepper.

3 **MEANWHILE, MAKE THE MEATBALLS** Preheat the oven to 350° and set a rack over a large rimmed baking sheet. In a large bowl, whisk the egg with the milk. Stir in the tortilla chips, cheese, garlic, oregano, 1½ teaspoons of salt and 1 teaspoon of pepper. Add the ground pork and beef and knead gently to combine.

4 Form the meat into 1½-inch meatballs and transfer them to the rack. Roast for 25 to 30 minutes, until the meatballs are browned and cooked through.

5 Add the meatballs to the sauce; toss carefully to coat. Transfer the meatballs to bowls and serve with warm tortillas.

MAKE AHEAD *The meatballs can be refrigerated in the sauce for up to 2 days. Reheat gently before serving.*

Stupak created this light, airy egg white frittata because he wanted to offer a brunch dish at Empellón Cocina that was healthy yet still delicious. To serve alongside, he makes a warm salsa ranchera *(Spanish for "ranch-style sauce") by blending roasted tomatoes, garlic and jalapeños.*

EGG WHITE & SPINACH FRITTATA WITH SALSA RANCHERA

TOTAL *40 min*   **MAKES** *4 servings*

4 *plum tomatoes*
2 *unpeeled garlic cloves*
2 *jalapeños*
2 *tablespoons extra-virgin olive oil*
Kosher salt and freshly ground pepper
1 *small white onion, minced*
5 *ounces baby spinach*
1 *dozen large egg whites, lightly beaten*

1 Preheat a large cast-iron skillet or griddle. Add the tomatoes, garlic cloves and jalapeños and roast over high heat, turning occasionally, until softened and charred in spots, about 12 minutes. Transfer to a plate to cool. Remove the stems and seeds from the jalapeños and add them to a blender along with the tomatoes. Peel the garlic and add it to the blender. Pulse to form a coarse salsa.

2 Preheat the oven to 325°. In a medium saucepan, heat 1 tablespoon of the olive oil until shimmering. Add the onion and cook over moderate heat, stirring occasionally, until golden, about 5 minutes. Add the salsa and simmer over moderately low heat for 15 minutes, stirring occasionally. Season with salt and pepper and keep warm.

3 Meanwhile, in a large ovenproof nonstick or cast-iron skillet, heat the remaining 1 tablespoon of olive oil until shimmering. Add the spinach and cook over moderate heat, tossing, until just wilted, about 2 minutes. Pour the egg whites over the spinach and season with salt and pepper. Transfer the skillet to the oven and bake the egg whites for 12 to 15 minutes, until just set. Serve the frittata with the salsa.

MAKE AHEAD *The salsa can be refrigerated for up to 5 days. Warm before serving.*

"These are the best pancakes you will ever have," Stupak says. They're light, fluffy and full of corn flavor from the masa harina (corn flour). The recipe is from his wife, Lauren Resler, the pastry chef at the Empellón restaurants.

BUTTERMILK PANCAKES WITH MASA HARINA

TOTAL *30 min*　　**MAKES** *about ten 5-inch pancakes*

¾　cup all-purpose flour
¾　cup masa harina (see Note)
2　tablespoons sugar
½　teaspoon salt
½　teaspoon baking powder
½　teaspoon baking soda
2　large eggs
2　cups buttermilk
3　tablespoons unsalted butter,
　　melted
Vegetable oil, for brushing
Butter and pure maple syrup,
　　for serving

1 In a large bowl, whisk the flour with the masa, sugar, salt, baking powder and baking soda. In another bowl, whisk the eggs with the buttermilk and melted butter, then whisk into the dry ingredients just until incorporated; add a tablespoon of buttermilk if the batter is very thick.

2 Preheat a griddle and brush lightly with oil. Scoop ⅓-cup-size mounds of batter onto the griddle, allowing them to spread on their own. Cook over moderate heat until bubbles appear on the surface, about 4 minutes. Flip and cook the pancakes until they are risen and golden brown on the bottom, about 2 minutes longer. Transfer to plates and serve hot with butter and maple syrup.

NOTE *Masa harina (nixtamalized corn flour) is available at supermarkets, specialty food shops and online at mexgrocer.com.*

RECIPE INDEX

CONTRIBUTORS

RECIPES

nicolaus balla
Bar Tartine, 561 Valencia St., San Francisco;
415-487-1600; *bartartine.com*

jimmy bannos, jr.
The Purple Pig, 500 N. Michigan Ave., Chicago;
312-464-1-PIG; *thepurplepigchicago.com*

julianne jones & didier murat
Vergennes Laundry, 247 Main St., Vergennes,
VT; 802-870-7157; *vergenneslaundry.com*

belinda leong
B. Patisserie, San Francisco; (Facebook)
b.patisserie; (Twitter) @b_patisserie

nico monday & amelia o'reilly
The Market Restaurant, 33 River Rd.,
Gloucester, MA; 978-282-0700; *themarket
restaurant.com*

bryant ng
The Spice Table, 114 S. Central Ave., Los
Angeles; 213-620-1840; *thespicetable.com*

sarah simmons
City Grit, 38 Prince St., New York City;
citygritnyc.com

justin smillie
Il Buco Alimentari e Vineria, 53 Great
Jones St., New York City; 212-837-2622;
ilbucovineria.com

michael solomonov
Zahav, 237 St. James Pl., Philadelphia;
215-625-8800; *zahavrestaurant.com*

alex stupak
Empellón Cocina, 105 First Ave., New York
City; 212-780-0999; Empellón Taqueria, 230
W. Fourth St., New York City; 212-367-0999;
empellon.com

RECIPE PHOTOS

christina holmes
A Michigan native now residing in New York
City, Holmes took all the full-page food photos
in this book. She has also contributed to
the Cooking Channel, *Whole Living* and *Marie
Claire*. *christinaholmesphotography.com*

PORTRAITS AND INTERIOR PHOTOS

dustin aksland
MICHAEL SOLOMONOV AT ZAHAV, PAGE 202
An internationally exhibited photographer
based in Brooklyn, New York, Aksland has contributed to magazines such as *Dwell, Esquire*
and *Travel + Leisure*. *dustinaksland.com*

cedric angeles
NICO MONDAY AND AMELIA O'REILLY AT THE
MARKET RESTAURANT, PAGE 106
Angeles describes his photographic style as
"honest, with no gimmicks." His work has
appeared in *Rolling Stone, Food & Wine* and
W. *cedricangeles.com*

leela cyd
BELINDA LEONG IN SAN FRANCISCO, PAGE 82
Based in Portland, Oregon, and Southern
California, Cyd has contributed to the *New
York Times, Chicago Tribune* and *Portland
Monthly*. *leelacyd.com*

corey hendrickson
JULIANNE JONES AND DIDIER MURAT AT
VERGENNES LAUNDRY, PAGE 58
Inspired by the people and landscape of
Vermont, where he lives, Hendrickson has con-
tributed to publications such as *Yankee* and
Smithsonian. *coreyhendrickson.com*

ethan hill
ALEX STUPAK AT EMPELLÓN COCINA AND
EMPELLÓN TAQUERIA, PAGE 226
New York City photographer Hill specializes
in portraits, which have been published in
Esquire, Food & Wine and *Newsweek*, among
other publications. *ethanhill.com*

peden + munk
BRYANT NG AT THE SPICE TABLE, PAGE 130
Taylor Peden and Jen Munkvold work as the
photo team PEDEN + MUNK. Their intimate
and provocative images have appeared
in many magazines, including *Vogue Spain,
House Beautiful* and *GQ*. *pedenmunk.com*

daniel shea
JIMMY BANNOS, JR., AT THE PURPLE PIG, PAGE 34
Shea, the subject of an exhibition at Chicago's
Museum of Contemporary Photography, has
contributed to magazines such as the *Atlantic,
Time* and *Wired*. *danielpshea.com*

michael turek
SARAH SIMMONS AT CITY GRIT, PAGE 154;
JUSTIN SMILLIE AT IL BUCO ALIMENTARI
E VINERIA, PAGE 178
Based in Brooklyn, New York, Turek calls his
photographic approach "stylized documen-
tary." His work has appeared in several
magazines, among them *Garden & Gun, Food
& Wine* and *Departures*. *turekphotography.com*

eric wolfinger
NICOLAUS BALLA AT BAR TARTINE, PAGE 10
Formerly a cook and baker, Wolfinger styled
and photographed the cookbook *Tartine
Bread* by Chad Robertson. He has also contributed to *Martha Stewart Living, Art Culinaire*
and *San Francisco,* among other publications.
ericwolfinger.com

FOOD&WINE
BOOKS

More books from
FOOD & WINE

Annual Cookbook
More than 700 recipes from the world's best cooks, including celebrity chefs like Rick Bayless, David Chang, Jamie Oliver and Jean-Georges Vongerichten.

Best of the Best
In one definitive volume, 115 tantalizing recipes from the best cookbooks of the year, chosen by FOOD & WINE. Authors include Jacques Pépin, Bobby Flay, Mario Batali and Nancy Silverton.

Cocktails
Over 140 incredible cocktail recipes and dozens of fantastic dishes from America's most acclaimed mixologists and chefs, plus an indispensable guide to cocktail basics and the top bars and lounges around the country.

Wine Guide
An essential, pocket-size guide focusing on the world's most reliable producers, with an easy-to-use food pairing primer.

TO ORDER, CALL 800-284-4145
OR LOG ON TO **foodandwine.com/books**